Contents

ii

Masculine and feminine: differentiation and integration*

Lucy Holmes

In this paper the author presents her theory of the woman's "internal triangle," a psychic structure based on the parents as self-objects. She illuminates her theory with case examples that illustrate how the triangle plays out in relation to pregnancy, childbirth, and early motherhood and describes ways in which integration of the internal triangle occurs throughout a woman's lifetime. She also addresses the Freudian notion of penis envy and female empowerment.

Freud (1912) famously said that "anatomy is destiny" (p. 189), and according to the great man, if your destiny is not to have a penis, you are out of luck. Freud (1905) believed that little children of both sexes have the theory that there is one genital and that genital is male because they can see the penis and the clitoris, but the ovaries and womb are invisible. Children react to this fact by assuming that the boy's penis is bigger and better and that the girl functions as a "little man." Freud (1932) thought that the little girl's symbolic castration had all sorts of unpleasant consequences: she was never really able to get over her oedipal conflict; her superego was anemic; and most horrible of all, she had no real capacity to love since all her energy was focused on being loved. No wonder then that feminists in the 1970s took aim at Freud as a destructive and misguided male chauvinist pig. I can remember that as a young student at

*This paper is a modified version of a paper presented at the Center for Modern Psychoanalytic Studies conference, "Sex and the Psyche," New York, December 6, 2008.

the Center for Modern Psychoanalytic Studies back in the '80s, I balked at the concept of penis envy. Eventually, I had to reluctantly accept the idea. My change of heart came about through examining my own penis envy in my analysis and also in the observation of my daughter, who came home from nursery school one day dismal and outraged. "Mom," she said, "James can pee standing up." I said, "Yes, but you get to wear panties with ruffles on them." She thought about that and then shook her head sadly, "It's not enough," she said.

And indeed it isn't. The penis gives the male sex all sorts of advantages. One of the most important of those advantages is that the penis helps little boys separate from the original preoedipal mother—that engulfing and omnipotent figure that all human beings must free themselves from if they are to mature and become independent (Chodorow, 1978). The penis is manifest evidence that "I am not my mother," and is enormously useful in helping boys to escape from the merged symbiosis of the preoedipal period. The boy clearly has something that the mother does not, and when his oedipal conflict is resolved, he can use his identification with his father to devalue and deny any identification at all with his mother. Freud (1925) stated that the oedipal conflict in boys is "literally smashed to pieces" (p. 257). What is totally obliterated in boys is the maternal introject that was incorporated with mother's milk in the preoedipal period. At the end of the boy's oedipal period, "I do not desire my mother" often becomes "I am nothing like my mother and cannot identify with her in any way." This idea promotes a dualistic way of thinking, with man as subject and woman as object. Now, for boys, there is an "I" and an "it" (Wilbur, 2000, pp. 110–111). This dynamic is responsible for ways of thinking that we associate with masculinity. It means that a tendency toward male chauvinism and the domination of women is born anew in each male human being. This is a dynamic that feminists need to understand in their attempts to liberate women. The oppression of women is cultural in many ways, but in a far deeper and more important way, it is set up in the human psyche very early in life. We all, men and women, have an unconscious impulse to control and subordinate the female sex because our first object in this world is a powerful woman who can feed us or let us die. We all have to find our own ways to subdue and control this loved and hated figure, and boys and girls find different solutions to this universal problem. I will discuss the female solution later, but first I want to emphasize that the male solution has some positive as well as negative aspects. The dualism set up by forever seeing self as subject and woman as object gives men a strong sense of right and wrong, a clearheaded, logical way of thinking that is less tainted with the primitive emotions associated with the preoedipal period and a strong investment in the healthy phallic energy that built the Taj Mahal and invented the airplane.

Freud (1924) thought that girls never really get over their penis deficiency and that their symbolic castration is the focal point of female development and female pathology. He even thought that the feminine desire for a baby was only a disguised wish for a penis.

When I went through pregnancy and childbirth, particularly when that birth experience wasn't obliterated by becoming a medical rather than a spiritual event, I felt in some ways that I had grown my own penis. I felt very empowered. And I had the idea, just a murky intuition at first, that childbirth had changed my mind. By that I mean that I came out of the experience with a different psyche from the one I had coming into it. I began to believe that, like adolescence, childbirth is a developmental milestone for women. As a result, I decided to study pregnancy and childbirth in my doctoral work. For two years I ran two psychotherapy groups for women. These groups consisted of pregnant women or women for whom pregnancy was a burning issue; that is, they desperately wanted a baby and were having trouble conceiving, or they were approaching their fortieth birthday and realizing that delaying having a child would soon mean they would never have one. For two years, I studied these women. One of the most striking things I observed was the number of ghosts in the room. When you sit with a pregnant woman, she is there, but so is her mother and her father and her fetus. Women consistently experienced pregnancy as "becoming my mother," and if this idea was too repellent, they were often infertile. If a woman had made a stronger identification with father than with mother, she often verbalized ambivalence about pregnancy, or sometimes conscious refusal to consider bearing a child. If a woman was already pregnant, her fetus was definitely there in the room too, usually as an object of projection. The unborn baby was alternately experienced as like another object in a woman's life—mother, father, or perhaps partner—or it was experienced as an aspect of the self. If a parent had been perceived as ruthless or parasitic, the fetus was often experienced as feeding on its mother in a way that would destroy her. If a woman suffered from a lack of self-esteem, she frequently was convinced that her baby was defective or deformed, like the devalued self. When the unborn baby was the object of love from the mother, it was seen as the mother's own best self, her ego-ideal.

Bollas (1992) wrote about "the ghosts within us," the internal objects that influence us (p. 56). He described these internal objects as highly condensed psychic textures, the traces of our encounters with the object world (p. 59). Listening to the themes played out in different ways in the minds of the women I worked with, I began to speculate that there is a strong tendency in women to internalize their parents. All these women in their own unique way seemed to be dealing on a fantasy level with an internal triangle of mother, father, and self. I also noticed that often the self, the woman's own ego, seemed to be oppressed by the fantasies surrounding the internal mother and father. I listened over and over as a drama involving these three intrapsychic characters unfolded within each woman according to her own unique script. I observed, as well, that the object within, the unborn baby, became the receptacle for all the projected fantasies involved in this script. A woman who described her dominating father as "a male chauvinist pig" was told by the doctors that her baby was a boy. She became obsessed with the idea that this baby was going to control and dominate her life, destroy her career, and turn her into a housewife. She had projected her father's attributes onto her unborn baby. Another woman, whose mother had gotten her addicted to crack cocaine when she was 13, was pregnant with her seventh child. She was able to stay away from drugs only when she was pregnant and nursing, and she was terrified because she had been diagnosed with lupus, and her obstetrician had told her that this must be her last pregnancy. "My babies protect me. I can be good when I'm pregnant," she explained. She had projected a good and protecting mother onto each unborn baby, and that fantasy had enabled her to be drug free.

These projected fantasies were consistently present in the pregnant women I worked with. Even more fascinating to me was the fact that as the women began to give birth, there was a significant shift in the internal triangle. Before giving birth, the women seemed subordinated to the internalized mother and father, but the female self gained significant ego strength in the process of birth, especially if the experience was not masked by drugs and technology. I saw again and again that enormous psychic development occurred when the fetus, so often the focus of the internal drama, was pushed out into the world. This transition from inner fantasy world to outer reality consistently gave women a sense of empowerment. The infant, the repository of so many primitive fantasies and projections, could now be seen, held, controlled, and nurtured. In this triumphant transition, the mother's ego was greatly strengthened. The new mother was able to identify with her own mother in a new way, not as the oppressed, humiliated mother who was the heir of the oedipal conflict, but as the life-giving, omnipotent mother of the preoedipal period. This, I decided, is why childbirth is truly a developmental milestone (Holmes, 2008).

It was at this point that I began to wonder why all these women I worked with demonstrated over and over the lively triangularity that inhabited their psyches. How did the internal triangle get set up? What purpose did it serve? I decided to study various authors, beginning with Freud and Klein, to see what they had to say about early female development. I was struck by a Kleinian idea that in the preoedipal and oedipal periods children, on a fantasy level, introject early objects. According to Klein (1946), this internalization serves both the life and death instincts. It is both an act of love, a wish to retain and identify with the object, and an act of hate, a wish to eat the object and destroy it. Most importantly, it is an attempt to gain control and mastery over an essentially uncontrollable object. It suddenly occurred to me that since a little girl lacks a penis that would prove she is not her mother, she can introject the mother. If she fantasizes that mommy is in her, she has both eaten her up and gained mastery over her frightening power. That is an elegant solution to a uniquely feminine problem. Boys separate by disidentifying with mother, but girls don't have that option. To separate from an object with whom she identifies, the girl incorporates the power of mother with her milk. Mommy is now inside rather than outside, and the girl has gained enormous control. Three-year-old girls demonstrate this fantasy of "mommy in me" with their dolls and their little baby carriages, while adult women in analysis verbalize the internalized mother.

Almost all of the female patients I have worked with also demonstrate a strong identification with their fathers. This identification may be healthy or pathological, but it is undisputedly present. As I studied the writings of authors like Benjamin (1988) and Chodorow (1978) about women and their fathers, I began to think about the difficulty of the oedipal period for the female sex. The humiliations of the oedipal defeat are especially challenging for little girls. Both boys and girls must relinquish the desire to have sex with the parent of the opposite sex during the oedipal period. But boys are offered a reward for the sacrifice of their incestuous wishes, i.e., an identification with phallic power: I, like father, have a penis, and I can control and subordinate mother. Little girls have no such bonus. Not only are they denied father's penis and with it any hope of receiving a baby from him, they are also denied access to any identification with the penis itself, that symbol of power and autonomy. Girls find themselves truly organless at the end of the oedipal period. They have no breasts, no womb with a baby in it, and no penis. In the face of this multifaceted mortification, it makes sense that the female child would again use introjection to internalize the father, and for the same reason that she internalized the mother. If the object is inside rather than outside, she can freely discharge libido and aggression toward it; in short, she gains control.

Though the introjection of the powerful father achieves the same thing that the earlier maternal introjection accomplished, it is not quite the same. When the female infant incorporated the mother, it was a very primitive pre-identification, a fantasy of ingesting mother with her milk. The imago introjected was a powerful woman with protruding, life-giving breasts, not the castrated, humiliated woman of the post-oedipal period. The introjection of the father is a more sophisticated operation, more of a true identification. The more mature and reality-oriented little girl of the post-oedipal period internalizes not only the imago of the father, but also his feelings and behaviors. Since it is very likely that the father, because of his own difficulties becoming masculine, has an unconscious or conscious tendency to devalue women, this devaluation is internalized within the female psyche. The introjection of the father makes the internal triangle complete, but it also totally alters the fantasized imago of the mother. When mother was originally introjected, she was a powerful object with phallic breasts. When father arrives on the intrapsychic scene, the introjected mother is subordinated and subdued, becoming the deficient, castrated figure that Freud associated with femininity. Within the complex endopsychic world of the female mind, father attacks mother, and both parents unconsciously subordinate and denigrate the self. Herein lie the seeds of female masochism (Holmes, 2008).

I am convinced that my theory of the internal triangle is a good one because, for one thing, it explains the facts well. It helps us understand all those attributes, both positive and negative, that we attribute to femininity. A triadic unconscious gives women an enormous capacity for identification, a rich inner life of imagination and intuition, and a capacity to sacrifice self for the other that insures that many marriages work and most newborns don't starve or die. That's the good news. The bad news is that the internal triangle is also implicated in some of the less admirable qualities of the truly feminine woman. Deutsch (1944, 1945), in her comprehensive work on female psychology, declared that women are passive, masochistic, and narcissistic. I believe the tendency to masochism results from the fact that the fantasized internal triangle is never equilateral. Mother with her protruding belly and life-giving breasts and father with his penis possess powers that the little girl, who feels organless until her own puberty, doesn't have. This internal subordination sets women up to masochistically attack the self. Female passivity, as described by Deutsch, is aggression turned upon the self. I believe this passivity is facilitated by the tendency of the female ego to feel attacked by the internalized mother and father. Female narcissism is actually a triumph of self-love against the powerful internalized parents, and it is of tremendous help to women in their difficult journey toward healthy femininity.

Freud (1932) asserted that women have weak superegos. The more recent work of Gilligan (1982) has, however, reframed that concept. It is not that women have less morality than men; they just think of it in a different way. Whereas men tend to define right and wrong in terms of logic and rules, women tend to see morality in the context of relationship. Men tend to be dualistic—either you're right or you're wrong; women tend to look at things from several points of view. A masculine morality says if you rob a bank, you go to jail. A feminine observer would want to know if the bank robber was desperate to feed his family. This ability to see things from several different points of view is also a derivative of the triangularity of the female unconscious.

Freud (1932) also felt that women lack the capacity to love, but let's look at the little girl's situation at the end of the oedipal period. The little girl has good reason to be furious with father for denying her a child and with mother for denying her a penis. But if she expresses her aggression directly or even experiences it consciously, she risks the loss of her feminine identity with mother and her hope of ever receiving a penis and a baby. Her destiny is to become passive, to mute the aggression and turn it toward the self. Her best choice is to await the time when she will receive a penis and a baby from someone like father. It is not, as Freud contended, that women can't love; they are given no choice. They can neither suckle their mothers nor penetrate their fathers. Their active loving has no external port and must, like their aggression, be turned back on the self. This redirection of libido and aggression infuses the female ego with the healthy narcissism that Deutsch (1944, 1945) described. Because she has no penis, breasts, or child in her womb on which to focus her narcissism, she tends to love herself more globally. Her entire body, as well as the products of her mind, her thoughts and feelings, becomes eroticized, giving the female personality its sensuality and emotional richness.

Clinical examples

The internal triangle is a useful theory not only because it explains a lot of facts well, but also because it has been of tremendous help to me in understanding my female patients. I developed the theory 10 years ago as a working hypothesis, but it continues to be confirmed in what women say to me today. If the internal triangle is too oppressive, the clinical picture is a masochistic woman so imprisoned in her identifications that she is clueless about her own thoughts and feelings. Often, she is unconsciously angry at the person with whom she is totally identified. For example, my patient Elise, an anorexic who was a compulsive caretaker and helper in my women's group, was so committed to being understanding and self-sacrificing that she neglected herself. She obsessively mothered the other group members, even when they were angry and attacking her. Elise described her own mother as a very sad and unhappy person. Her mother was so immersed in her own misery that she badly neglected Elise. In unconscious identification with her mother, Elise neglected herself in my group, even seeming to enjoy being abused by other members. Her obsessive helpfulness and empathy defended her against a powerful longing to be taken care of. Elise talked about her mother as a gentle victim. But after hearing about the tyranny of this victim for many weeks, the other women in Elise's group began to feel angry at her mother, and they invited Elise to be angry too. Elise said:

> Angry? I can't be angry at my mother. It's like attacking myself. It's like we're one person. I don't know where I end, and she begins. She's inside me. I was always the one who took care of my mother. She used to wash dishes without gloves, and her hands were blistered and cracked, and she loved it. She loved pain. She was always cutting her fingers and burning herself in the kitchen. It was a form of self-mutilation. Eating was torture. Every bite she put in her mouth, she talked about how fattening it was. And I'm like her. Even the things I enjoy, my ballet dancing, I do it till I'm abusing myself, like my mother.

Elise was so identified with her difficult mother that she couldn't even entertain the idea that she might be angry about her mother's neglect and masochistic suffering. In the here and now of the group, Elise compulsively identified with and took care of the other members so that she would never experience her own aggression.

Another of my patients, Gretchen, is oppressed by her father introject. Gretchen would be horrified to hear this analysis of her unconscious because she hates her father, who abused her and her mother for many years, not only verbally but physically. Gretchen's father had the macho idea that wives and daughters must submit and obey, and constantly told Gretchen's mother how stupid she was. He became enraged if his wife or his children dared to disagree with him. "His truth was the only truth," Gretchen said. Gretchen managed to escape her childhood environment and to get a law degree and a doctorate in mathematics. When she came into treatment, she was 37 years old. She had never had a good relationship with a man, but very much wanted to have a baby. She said, "I've spent my whole life proving I'm smart, but now I want to be a mother." Gretchen was skeptical about treatment. She wondered if I was smart enough to help her. She wanted answers from me, but when I told her the answer was for her to say everything, she told me that was a ridiculous idea. She demeaned every word that came out of my mouth, but when I was silent, she told me that I bored her. She talked about the men who asked her out on a date in terms of their parts: his ears were too big; his penis was too small. If a man she was dating said one thing that she didn't agree with, she decided that he was not smart enough for her. She was mystified because every man she got involved with managed to escape. Gretchen has been in treatment now for five years, and she is involved with a man who says he would like to get married and have a family. The sex is great, but they fight constantly. They attack and are sarcastic to each other. Gretchen has told me that she wants to keep this man, "Somehow he makes me feel safe and loved, and he wants to marry me. I want to be married once before I get old." I asked her if it would be possible to give herself an order to say positive and loving things to him whenever she has a positive feeling toward him. She was astonished at this idea and replied, "It's very hard for me to say loving things toward men. It's much easier to be belittling and sarcastic." Gretchen is getting close to a conscious awareness that she operates in a world under the control of that difficult father who demeaned and abused everyone. Though she consciously hates her father, her unconscious has identified with his power, domination, and monopoly on intellect.

The internal triangle manifests itself in the treatment room in a myriad of ways. Many women perceive reality as if they were in the mind of their own mother. This idea came to me in working with a patient who suffers from terrible anxiety attacks. When she is in the throes of an attack, she weeps and threatens suicide. She tells me she is going to end up poor and alone on the street. She will be manipulated by her ex-husband until the day she dies, and there is nothing she can do about it. Though she presents herself as a helpless victim during these attacks, her eyes look narrow and angry, and I feel assaulted by her hysterical, inarticulate crying. Once, she sat up on the couch and said to me in a rage, "Do I have a sign on me that says 'Abuse me!'?" When she did this, I felt that I was her abuser, that she was trying to kill me, and that I wanted to kill her in return. A few months later when we were enduring one of these storms of rage and grief, she put her hands to her face and said in despair, "I am in the mind of my mother!" When I asked her what she meant by that, she said, "All this is not me. I feel like I'm trapped inside my mother's mind and can't get out." This woman professes hate for her mother, who has been dead for many years. Her first memory is of her mother telling her she deserved nothing. Her mother made her clean bathrooms and scrub floors from the age of five and beat my patient when she didn't do a good job. Consciously, my patient expresses nothing but aggression toward this hateful mother, but she seems to be telling me that she can only perceive reality from her mother's point of view. Though she sees herself as a helpless victim, when she is in the middle of one of her anxiety attacks, she assaults herself and me in the same way her mother tortured her. Her fears of being evicted and out in the snow confirm her mother's idea that she deserves nothing. Once I said to this patient, "Your mother may be dead, but she has a three-room apartment in your unconscious." She laughed at that, and it seemed to help her realize that she can be as sadistic to herself and to me as her mother was to her.

Since my patient described her reality as the mind of her mother, I have listened for this dynamic in other women. A beautiful and privileged woman that I work with was an unwanted baby and an unloved child. Her mother loved to tell her three daughters that she never should have had children and that her happiness ended when they were born. My patient has a rich husband who loves her, beautiful children, and great talent as a singer. She is constantly going out to lunch, making tennis dates, and throwing parties. Yet she describes herself as friendless and as "a piece of shit" and her life as a sewer. Reality for her is the mind of her mother: she should never have been born. Another patient, whose mother was an obsessive perfectionist, lives her life in a state of perpetual anxiety: the plane is going to crash; the food she prepares for a dinner party will be less than perfect. This patient said to me, "I can attach my anxiety to anything. It's not connected to reality." I asked what would happen if she just put it down for a while. She said, "Oh, no! I need it. If I put it down, even for a minute, I would leave here, go out on the street, and bam! I'd be run over by a taxi!" Again, the mind of the mother, a maternal introject that unconsciously attacks the self.

In addition to being oppressed by an internalized father or mother, many women struggle with a conflict between masculine and feminine identifications. Naomi was a pregnant woman who tortured herself throughout her pregnancy about becoming her mother, who never had a career and devoted her entire life to her children. Naomi loved this mother dearly, even idealized her. She said she became pregnant so easily because she admired and identified with her mother. But she saw her mother as oppressed. She served the father and her children in a totally self-sacrificing way. As a child, Naomi wanted to be like her father who had a successful business and all the authority at home. Naomi had gotten an M.B.A.; she wore her hair very short and refused to wear skirts because they made her feel powerless. She told me that if the baby was a girl, she would never let it play with a doll. "I'll give her fire trucks and scooters," she said. Throughout her pregnancy, Naomi struggled with her masculine and feminine identifications. But after her son was born, she said, "You know, I've been thinking. Womanhood is a wonderful thing. Have I ever really allowed myself to feel like a woman? Maybe it isn't such a horrible thing to let little girls play with dolls. It doesn't mean she can't drive a truck or have a career too."

After giving birth, Naomi was able to embrace and integrate both her masculine and feminine identifications. She identified with her mother in a new way, not as an oppressed victim, but as a powerful creator and nurturer of life. She enjoyed nursing her baby. But when he was a year old, she was able to call upon her father introject and go back to work on Wall Street and get a promotion.

Conclusion

This integration of the masculine and feminine is an important goal in psychoanalysis, whether the patient is male or female. I think male development and female development are very different, but I also want to emphasize that these differences are tendencies, not absolutes. There are plenty of masculine women and men who have feminine skills—quite a few in the profession of psychoanalysis. Male psychoanalysts are almost always very talented at identifying and empathizing. Lots of female analysts write books, found institutes and organizations, and are happy to consider themselves ambitious and competitive. We can explore male and female differences without denigrating either sex. Indeed, we need to value both the masculine and the feminine if we are to evolve and grow as a species. We can say that men tend, because of the challenges they face in the preoedipal and oedipal periods, to stress individuality, rights, and justice. Phallic energy insures that we continue to have sex and that the enemy and game are killed when we need to survive. This phallic energy explored the earth and the heavens, developed culture, ethics, and law, and launched rockets. The masculine tendency toward duality, toward seeing oneself as a subject and the rest of the world as an object invented science and medicine. An "I" looking at an "it" through a microscope discovered bacteria and DNA. This is a positive energy, and human beings, whether male or female, need to find that energy within themselves to have meaningful lives. Women, for reasons I have tried to enumerate, tend to emphasize relationship, complexity, and nurturance. I believe it is this feminine tendency that will ultimately save our environment and bring peace to the Middle East. Freud described women as deficient men, but lately there has been a tendency to define men as deficient women. This is just an unfortunate reversal of the sexism that feminists have been railing against for over 200 years. We need both perspectives to face the challenges of the modern world. It is good to explore difference and then to find ways to integrate what is best in order to move forward. This integration is vital if we are to help our patients develop and grow. Whatever has been repressed, whether masculinity or femininity, needs to be made conscious and integrated into the personality.

This integration is also essential to the profession of psychoanalysis itself. When we think in a dualistic, masculine way, we study our patients objectively and create drive theory and new ideas about human development. When we utilize the feminine perspective, we realize that although theory is useful, every human being who comes for treatment is a complex and unique person, not just an "it" to whom we apply our science. Through the feminine tendencies of identification, intuition, and nurturance, we meet each new patient with a mind that does not impose any theory on that patient, but opens itself up to what is before us in the here and now of the session. The masculine and the feminine—we need them both to be successful analysts.

While we were discussing penis envy in a class I taught at the Center for Modern Psychoanalytic Studies, a young woman said, "It's not so much that I would rather have a penis than a vagina; I want them both." Well, I say, why not? Exploring and enjoying the integration of the masculine and the feminine in our patients, ourselves, and the profession of psychoanalysis can be a unifying and life-enhancing experience.

references Benjamin, J. (1988), *The Bonds of Love: Psychoanalysis, Feminism, and the Problem of Domination.* New York: Pantheon Books.

Bollas, C. (1992), *Being A Character: Psychoanalysis and Self-experience.* New York: Hill and Wang.

Chodorow, N. (1978), *The Reproduction of Mothering: Psychoanalysis and the Sociology of Gender.* Berkeley: University of California Press.

Deutsch, H. (1944), *The Psychology of Women: A Psychoanalytic Interpretation.* Vol. I. New York: Grune and Stratton.

Deutsch, H. (1945), *The Psychology of Women: A Psychoanalytic Interpretation.* Vol. II. New York: Grune and Stratton.

Freud, S. (1905), Three essays on the theory of sexuality. *Standard Edition.* London: Hogarth Press, 7:125–245.

Freud, S. (1912), On the universal tendency to debasement in the sphere of love. *Standard Edition.* London: Hogarth Press, 11:177–190.

Freud, S. (1924), The dissolution of the Oedipus complex. *Standard Edition.* London: Hogarth Press, 19:171–180.

Freud, S. (1925), Some psychical consequences of the anatomical distinction between the sexes. *Standard Edition.* London: Hogarth Press, 19:241–258.

Freud, S. (1932), Femininity. Lecture XXXIII, New introductory lectures on psycho-analysis. *Standard Edition.* London: Hogarth Press, 22:112–135.

Gilligan, C. (1982), *In a Different Voice: Psychological Theory and Women's Development.* Cambridge: Harvard University Press.

Holmes, L. (2008), *The Internal Triangle: New Theories of Female Development.* New York: Jason Aronson.

Klein, M. (1946), Notes on some schizoid mechanisms. *International Journal of Psychoanalysis,* 27:99–110.

Wilbur, K. (2000), *A Brief History of Everything.* Boston: Shambhala Press.

52 East 78th Street
New York, New York 10075
lucyholmes@nyc.rr.com

The roles of anatomy and psyche in destiny: an integration of evolutionary psychology, neuroscience, and psychoanalysis*

Eugene B. Kalin

This paper explores the relationship between anatomy and psyche in relation to gender differences and offers a modification of Freud's perspective on gender differences. The author addresses the ways that biological forces—in particular those that impel us to reproduce—shape human identity along gender lines and influence psychic structure. Parallels between scientific research on arousal reduction circuits in the brain and Freudian drive theory are also examined.

In 1912 Freud made the famous statement that "anatomy is destiny" (p. 189). Because he believed sexual orientation to be constitutional, Freud held that there are masculine and feminine sexual and gender roles that are polar opposites and are unchanging. This paper examines Freud's notion from an evolutionary vantage with the idea that anatomy and psyche co-evolve. It follows from this that neither gender nor gender relations are inflexible categories. This topic is treated in three parts. First, some of the characteristics of human mating behavior that follow from evolutionary principles are examined, and evolutionary sex differences are delineated, suggesting there may be a natural animosity between the sexes due to

*This paper is a modified version of a paper presented at the Center for Modern Psychoanalytic Studies conference, "Sex and the Psyche," New York, December 6, 2008.

different biological and reproductive forces. Second, variations in gender identification between the sexes are examined by linking evolution to the development of psychic structure. These variations suggest that the evolved human faculty of an experiencing mind, along with the fact that females give birth, creates different mental pressure in males and females concerning their core identity and their need to establish psychic autonomy. Third, a connection is drawn between the scientific findings of arousal reduction circuits in the brain and Freudian drive theory, which, as a cultural development, circles back to evolution. These explorations lead to the conclusion that evolutionary processes have influenced the design of not only the body, but also the psyche, allowing a modification of Freud's explanation that gender orientation influences destiny.

Evolution

It is a basic premise of this paper that human behavior is motivated by thoughts and feelings—some conscious and some unconscious—reflecting instincts. This idea is in accord with the Freudian instinct theory model that there is a human nature in a Darwinian sense, and stands in contrast to the idea that the mind is a blank slate as viewed from the Lockean perspective, which maintains that all behavior is learned through experience or acquired through socialization, or the Hobbesian notion that every man is at war with every other man (Pinker, 2003, pp. 5–7). That there is a human nature in a Darwinian sense should be understood in the context of brain gene expression. Indeed, "there is increasing appreciation that *social information* can alter brain gene expression and behavior" (Robinson, Fernald & Clayton, 2008, p. 896; italics added). Genetic studies have documented sex differences that originated in human biology, and evolutionary psychology has provided a web of motives that entangle us in conflicts of interest with members of the opposite sex. Although men and women are capable of living together harmoniously, there is a natural antagonism due to physical and mental differences that result from evolutionary imperatives.

Within an evolutionary framework, the evidence states that males and females have distinct reproductive roles. Therefore, their sex drives have separate aims, and they develop different psychological strategies and tactics to achieve them. This leads to dissimilar perceptions and disparate viewpoints and defenses and thus to the "self-serving biases" to justify reproductive agendas (Pinker, 2003, p. 294). This dissimilarity impacts attitudes and beliefs and results, ultimately, in divergent approaches to relationships. Basically, men and women have evolved differently because they have different reproductive agendas. And these differences in the reproductive agendas mean that conflict, competition, and manipulation as well as romance, sexual harmony, and love play roles in human sexual psychology (Buss, 2003, p. 18). These ideas are basic to the evolutionary theory of sexual selection for reproductive advantage.

There are two major areas of controversy that have to be resolved to accept these contentions regarding gender differences: the first one is the well-known issue of psyche versus soma or nurture versus nature. The Freudian-Darwinian biological or materialist position is that anatomy is genetically selected, reflecting soma and designated by the terms "male" and "female." This clashes with the socio-cultural, postmodern orientation that states that all behavior is learned and acquired through experience and that gender roles are socially determined by assigning meaning to biological differences (Horney, 1937; Thompson, 1942). Taken to its extreme, this implies that no genes and chromosomes—essentially no biologically predetermined facts—are involved in gender.

The cultural and interpersonal model maintains that personality is formed around early relationships and that gender differences are "an artifact of social structures, most particularly inequalities in male-female participation in child rearing" (Mitchell & Black, 1995, p. 222). Chodorow states, "gender difference is not absolute, abstract or irreducible; it does not involve an essence of gender" (qtd. in Mitchell & Black, p. 222). The postmodern position is even more definitive as Gagnon states, "no tension exists between nature and culture because nature, as such, is purely a socially constructed category" (qtd. in Mitchell & Black, p. 223).

Freud believed that gender development was a corollary of sexual development. He felt that men and women have biologically dictated gender roles, stating, "it is quite impossible to adjust the claims of the sexual instinct to the demands of civilization" (1912, p. 190), and "The difference between the sexual development of males and females... [is a] consequence of the anatomical distinction between their genitals and of the psychical situation involved in it" (1925, pp. 256–257). He added that personality forms around sexuality in a "bedrock" of preexisting structure (1937, p. 253).

It is well known that Freud (1925) pronounced that the psychic consequences of the anatomical distinctions between the sexes take the form of different castration fears, different superego formations, and different oedipal pressures in the selection of a sexual object. He specified that men develop castration fears and contempt for women, while women repress their libido and develop penis envy and a sense of inferiority (pp. 241–258). Freud implied, however, that civilization is always working against the persistent biological drives dominated by sexuality (p. 257). In contrast to his statement that anatomy is destiny this would seem to indicate that he believed society can influence the sexual drive through learning. The basic issue, still disputed, is whether the social environment is the product of innate sexual instincts or whether sexual behavior is the product of the social environment.

The other controversy falls within the field of evolution. This pertains to the conflict between the individual and the species and forces a discrimination between individual survival adaptations and adaptations for the benefit of the species and indeed the putative role of the interaction between biology and culture. To shed more light on this issue, I will examine some of the principles of an evolutionary theory of mental phenomena and explore conflicting ideas in current theory in order to clarify some of the ambiguities surrounding sex and gender differences.

Some evolutionary oriented psychologists think of culture in terms of genes and in fact attribute an inheritance factor to culture. This school believes that "culture is shaped by the evolved information-processing properties of human brains" (Richerson & Boyd, 2005, p. 149). This model challenges "the doctrine that culture lives in a separate universe from brains, genes, and evolution" (Pinker, 2003, p. 60). Instead, it propounds that, due to language and consciousness, the human species has evolved a biology and a culture that continuously interact with and affect each other: "culture is crucial, but culture could not exist without mental facilities that allow humans to create and learn culture to begin with" (pp. viii–ix). Ridley (2003) states that "Human bodies are products of natural selection; but human minds and human behavior are products of 'culture'" (p. 175). He suggests that human nature reflects human culture, not the reverse: Grammatical language, hierarchy, romantic love, sexual jealousy, long-term bonds between the genders are "trainable instincts peculiar to our species and are just as surely the products of evolution as eyes and thumbs" (p. 175). Dawkins (1999) claims that there is no biological reason for expecting genetic influences to be any more significant or irreversible than environmental ones in having modifying effects on human development (p. 13). Lorenz (1966) and Dawkins (1999) both say that since culture is part of the human environment and can be considered to be an extended phenotype, culture is also a product of human nature and both are products of evolution.

From this point of view you can never be sure what in the human species is an instinct. There might be all sorts of cultural, economic, and political aspects to a behavior that are grounded in instinct. On the other hand, some behaviors may be purely cultural creations even though they appear to be universal and genetically selected (Jablonka & Lamb, 2005, p. 219). The distinction between cause and effect in the mating behavior between men and women is confounded. Thus, contrary to the popular understanding that inheritance is propagated by genes alone and that the social environment reflects gender alone, the co-evolution branch of evolutionary theorists hypothesize that there is an inextricable interaction between nature and nurture—that culture and human nature are embedded in each other (Jablonka & Lamb, 2005, p. 221). Miller (2000) cautions, however, that concepts such as "'gene-culture-co-evolution'" are speculative because they do not clarify the basic "fitness" principle of evolutionary biology and questions how this process promotes survival or reproduction (p. 28).

Some Freudian analysts consider that the instincts, which originate in the somatic matrix, organize mental processes and motivate behavior (see Freud, 1900; Fenichel, 1945; Green, 1998; Kernberg, 1988). In an evolutionary context human instincts are a consequence of adaptations since biological reproductive tendencies determine instincts. From the perspective of evolutionary biologists, the divergent psychic content of men and women is a reflection of different reproductive agendas resulting from sexual selection pressures and does not follow from either sexual development or gender differences. Evolutionary theory views the human mind and human nature as "a set of biological adaptations" and tries to elucidate "which problems of living and reproducing" (or what selection pressures) influenced these adaptations as species evolved over time to become adapted to their environment (Miller, 2000, p. 5). According to Miller, Darwin "argued that evolution is driven not just by natural selection for [individual] survival [advantage], but by an equally important process that he called sexual selection through mate choice" (p. 3). Sexual desire and mate choice are thus seen as driving forces in the mind's evolution. The idea that the human mind can be understood "as a courtship tool, evolved to attract . . . sexual partners," not a tool that adapted solely through natural selection for individual survival benefits, has been gaining increasing acceptance over time "because reproductive success is evolution's bottom line" (p. 4 & p. 5). In fact, it is hypothesized by evolutionary psychologists that once language developed in humans, "thought itself became subject to sexual selection" (p. 10).

It has also been hypothesized that linguistic ability and vocabulary size itself has been strongly shaped by sexual selection and that most of the words that we know have been learned not because they're useful for survival, but because they are useful for courtship (Miller, 2000, p. 375): "Language evolved as much to display our fitness as to communicate useful information" (p. 390). In other words, language evolved as a courtship device, rather than as an efficiency increasing, information processing system. The better model for the mind, as Miller notes, is as "an entertainment system designed to stimulate other brains" (p. 155).

Miller (2000) points out that the courtship ornaments and displays of our species are symbolic, including language, literature, music, art, sports, creativity, humor, religion, morality, and love, which incidentally happen to yield some survival benefits (p. 5). These are the human equivalents of the peacock's tail that make no sense as adaptations for individual survival, but make sense as adaptations for courtship that evolved to attract sexual partners, leading to reproduction and therefore survival of the species (pp. 138-176). For this reason, according to Miller, there are no "plausible survival payoffs" (p. 18) to language and consciousness, and sexual preference should be considered as a cause of evolution rather than an outcome (p. 6). He also says, "The brain benefits were mainly reproductive," i.e., people pick one another for their brains (p. 20). Indeed, Miller (Wikipedia, 2010) proposes that the adaptive features of the expressive aspects of human behavior "evolved through mutual mate-choice by both sexes to advertise intelligence, creativity, moral character and heritable fitness." Some of the "human mind's most distinctive features, such as our capacities for language, art [and] music," he states, "...fit [the] criteria [for heritability] quite well" (2000, p. 14). Along the same lines, Horvath (2000) notes: "The novel, the film, the quip, and the code of conduct are the human equivalents of the peacock's tail, elaborate examples of ornamentation that advertises fitness through their very excess and flagrant lack of utility" (p. 1). However, as Miller (2000) points out, sexual selection for attracting partners and selection for survival are distinct processes that have different consequences (p. 8). Environmental, physical, or biological factors often drive natural selection, whereas people, sexual rivals and mates, are the exclusive agents of sexual selection (p. 9).

Nevertheless, the theory that natural selection (rather than sexual selection, symbolic communication, or social functioning) drives evolutionary processes has many proponents (Fisher, 1930; Wright, 1932; Dobzhansky, 1937; Mayr, 1942; Haldane, 1957; Lieberman, 1984; Pinker, 1994; Richardson, 1998). The modern evolutionary synthesis, first propagated by Huxley (1942), uniting the mechanisms of natural selection with molecular genetics, adds credence to natural selection as the foundation of evolutionary theory. If language emerged under evolutionary pressure, then cognitive capacity developed in addition to here-and-now survival requirements. This has suggested what is called a general-intelligence hypothesis or domain-general model of adaptation that accounts for how humans solve non-recurrent problems of evolution in novel ways (Gottfredson, 2007, pp. 387–389). It posits that inference processes and reasoning procedures operate similarly irrespective of content and context. However, to fully understand the development of cognitive faculties to solve the recurrent problems of evolution, according to Hirschfeld and Gelman (1994), we must recognize that the mind is not an all-purpose problem solver, but consists of subsystems designed to perform circumscribed, domain-specific cognitive and psychological tasks (p. 4). From this perspective, Cosmides and Tooby (1994) indicate that humans are designed to solve problems that range from

> solicitation of assistance from one's parents, to language acquisition, to modeling the spatial distribution of local objects, to coalition formation and cooperation, to the deduction of intentions on the basis of facial expressions, to avoiding incest...to the interpretation of threats, to mate selection, [and] to object recognition. (p. 88)

Other hypotheses of the origins and functioning of the human brain include an adapted-intelligence hypothesis that posits that "particular mental faculties evolved in response to particular environmental changes" (Christakis & Fowler, 2009, p. 240) and a social-intelligence hypothesis or social network model that states that we "are adapted to a highly social environment" and that skills have evolved in humans to

> form particular social groups with particular social-network ties...[and] then transmit...their knowledge to others near and far. At some point in evolutionary history, primates applied the skills initially developed for finding a mate and maintaining a stable reproductive union to relationships that were not reproductive. (p. 241)

Another hypothesis of mental evolution has been proposed by Jaynes (1976). He states that consciousness is primarily learned although there may be adaptive reinforcements. He argues that the transition from the bicameral mind to subjective consciousness is of cultural origin, "learned on the basis of language and taught to others, rather than any biological necessity" (p. 220). However, he argues, this has survival value and may have been "assisted by a certain amount of natural selection...and those biologically most able to learn it would be most likely to survive" (pp. 220–221).

While "[s]exual selection is a theory of evolutionary function, not a theory of subconscious motivation" (Miller, 2000, p. 15), the development of consciousness, language, and symbolic thinking, along with the unconscious and instincts, is a theory of motivation. The Freudian concept of libido can be seen as reflecting a transformation of sexual selection imperatives, while aggression can be viewed as reflecting survival selection imperatives. Some feelings serve survival functions and some serve reproductive functions. The instinct for survival is usually subsumed under the sex drive in the psychoanalytic literature. However, although libido and aggression often fuse and are interdependent, as evolutionary adaptive mechanisms, the sexual instinct can be viewed primarily as a reproductive mechanism, and aggression can be viewed primarily as a self-preservation mechanism.

Sexual selection through mate choice may be viewed through a psychological lens because sexual choice and courtship are psychological activities. Evolutionary psychology doesn't reduce psychology to biology, "but sees psychology as a driving force in biological evolution" (Miller, 2000, p. 16). Sexual selection theory asserts that "big brains contributed to reproductive success...by enabling men to outwit and out scheme other men...because big brains were originally used to court and seduce members of the other sex" (Ridley, 2003, p. 21). Our brains grew so big and we became so intelligent not to make tools to gain a survival advantage or to anticipate events and plan, but to psychologically influence one another. Prehistoric social competition was played for sexual stakes in a form of warfare never before seen in the natural world; "psychological warfare" was waged with conversation, charm and wit and "Machiavellian tricks" to manipulate and deceive others (Miller, 2000, p. 13 & p. 6).

With the capacity for speech, the evolution of the faculty of consciousness expanded. The dimension of verbal thought was added to awareness. Humans could delay acting, behave symbolically, plan ahead, form concepts and ideas, and apply reason. Humans became self-aware and devised recursive thinking—thoughts about thoughts—so that an infinite variety of thoughts, intentions, and behaviors could be generated from a finite repertoire of adaptive input options.

In humans with language and consciousness, and the ability to symbolize drives, different reproductive functions are believed to have lead to different sexual strategies in males and females and concomitant psychic, instead of physical, conflict between them. Males and females could develop disparate viewpoints or defenses that symbolized or justified their reproductive drives. Typically, for example, a man might think, "Women are so controlling; they want to possess you," or "They are so demanding; they're never satisfied," while a woman might have the idea that, "Men are so immature; they want to have their cake and eat it," or "Men are so irresponsible; they can't make a commitment."

There is strong social pressure to minimize the psychological differences between men and women. However, to assume that men and women are psychologically the same goes against what is now known about evolved human sexual psychology. Under the influence of sexual selection, "under which each sex competes for access to desirable mates of the other sex, it would be astonishing to find that men and women were psychologically identical in aspects of mating" since they have faced different reproductive pressures for millions of years (Buss, 2003, p. 211).

Many sex differences, of course, have nothing to do with biology. Men and women are not born with indistinguishable minds. They differ in many ways other than anatomically. However, different does not mean unequal (Pinker, 2003, p. 343). Natural selection tends toward an equal investment in the two sexes, that is, toward equal, effective designs for survival. Being male or being female is an equally good strategy from the genetic point of view (pp. 343–346). Somewhere along the evolutionary continuum male and female transformed into man and woman, but the distinctions overlap and intertwine.

The sex drive within us may be much more specific in certain ways, however, than we like to acknowledge. The evidence from evolution is that men covet youth and physical attractiveness; women covet status, maturity, and economic success; men compete for opportunities to mate, and women choose the best quality men. It is no longer doubted that men and women differ in their preferences for a mate, in their proclivities for casual sex without emotional involvement, in their desire for sexual variety, and in the nature of their sexual fantasies (Buss, 2003, pp. 8–13). In addition, they differ in their tactics to attract mates, to keep mates, and to replace mates:

> Men and woman face different forms of interference with their preferred sexual behavior and so differ in the kinds of events that trigger their emotions such as anger and jealousy.... These differences between the sexes appear to be universal features of our evolved selves. They govern the relations between the sexes. (Buss, 2003, p. 211)

According to this viewpoint, since evolution operates by adaptations to meet sexual needs, different reproductive pressures naturally lead to conflict between the sexes because for each sex the other is a sought-after resource to be exploited. From this perspective, it seems reasonable to include sexual desire and sexual choice as an evolutionary force that could have shaped the human mind, just as biologists use sexual choice to explain the behavior of animals. There is a natural animosity and an irreducible antagonism due to different biological forces and different reproductive options and resources.

The theory of sexual selection states that "the goal of an animal is not just to survive but to breed" (Ridley, 2003, p. 20). In fact, since reproduction is the essential criteria for the propagation of genes and the continuation of a species, when breeding and individual survival come into conflict, breeding takes precedence. Ridley points out, "This goal is so central to life that it has influenced the design not only of the body but of the psyche" (p. 20). It can be inferred that Freud (1925) actually was referring to the issue of sexual selection when he stated that the development of the superego, in the form of conscience and morality, as heir to the resolution of the Oedipus complex is a "victory of the race over the individual" (p. 257). A victory of race can be understood as a victory for propagation of the species over survival of the individual. Further, if you substitute the words "sexual selection" for "the sexual function," in Freud's statement that "neurosis is based upon the struggle of the ego against the demands of the sexual function" (p. 257), this also can be understood as recognition of the survival and sexual selection conflict inherent in the struggle of the individual and the species.

Why do men and women battle over fidelity? Men often seek sexual access with a minimum of obligation and investment. They are extremely choosy and "stringently guard" their assets. While coveting this investment, "[t]he sexual access that men seek is precisely the resource that women are so selective about giving" (Buss, 2003, p. 144). If men are opportunists—polygamists at heart—Ridley (2003) asks, "[W]here does marriage come from?" He goes on to explain, "The two goals are contradictory only because women are not prepared to divide themselves neatly into wives and whores." Women are not the passive chattel of despots. They are "active adversar[ies] in the sexual chess game" and have their own goals. Women are far less interested in polygamy than men, "but that does not mean they are not sexual opportunists" (p. 212). Since men can improve reproductive success by philandering, it would be reasonable to expect that the nature of the human male is to "take advantage of opportunities for polygamy and that some of the things they do have that end in mind" (p. 193). Males use polygamous mating and "wealth, power, and violence as means to sexual ends in the competition with other men—though usually not at the expense of sacrificing a secure monogamous relationship" (p. 206).

According to Tucker (1993), an evolutionary reproductive imperative is responsible for the universal characteristic of "female coyness":

> [Since] males can spread their sperm far and wide, impregnating as many females as possible, while females may get only one mating opportunity per season...females must choose wisely. In almost every species, males are the sexual aggressors while females hold back, trying to select the best mate. (p. 30)

Why then are women ever unfaithful? Ridley (2003) notes that "[a] female human being does not have to share her sexual favors with many males to prevent infanticide," as do apes and monkeys. However, "she may have a good reason to share them with one well-chosen male apart from her husband" because her husband is most likely not the best male there is (p. 217). "His value is that he is monogamous and will therefore not divide his child-rearing effort among several families. But why accept his genes? Why not have his parental care and some other male's genes?" (p. 218). The fact that women are sometimes unfaithful can thus be explained by the idea that adultery may have played a big part in shaping human society because there have often been "advantages to both sexes from within a monogamous marriage in seeking alternative sexual partners." This implies that adultery is natural, that there is "some valid biological reason for seeking sex outside of marriage without abandoning the marriage—some instinct in women not to deny themselves the option of a sexual 'plan B' when plan A does not work out so well"(p. 219). In the game of sexual chess each adversary is using or exploiting the other for reproductive advantage. "The different costs and benefits of [adulterous] affairs for males and females explain most of the sex differences in human psychology" (Miller, 2000, p. 187).

Despite the clear reproductive advantages of polygamy, some species have turned to the more limiting system of monogamy. Why, asks Tucker (1993), is monogamy a successful format for human cooperation when it limits the possibility of men having as many mates as they desire and women having the best choice possible? Tucker explains that monogamy "reduces the sexual competition among males" by providing the possibility that every male gets a chance to mate. "As a result, the do-or-die quality of sexual competition among males abates. When one male can collect many females, mating takes on a deadly intensity" (p. 32). Monogamy is also better adapted to the task of rearing offspring. This is particularly true where the offspring go through a long period of dependency because "[t]he task is better handled by *two* parents than one. Quite literally, a species [may adopt] monogamy 'for the sake of the children'" (p. 32).

The unconscious sex instinct represents the evolutionary imperative. Males are adulterers and polygamists, but so are females although not to the same degree as males. Being polygamous achieves reproductive success for males, just as being monogamous does for women. Polygamy or adultery enables a male to have more young and to produce as many offspring as possible, and it enables a female to have better young and to produce the best offspring possible. However, "[f]emale animals gain little from sexual opportunism, for their reproductive ability is limited not by how many males they mate with but how long it takes to bear offspring. In this respect men and women are very different" (Ridley, 2003, p. 218).

Unless an evolutionary environment changes radically, it is believed that a species "can only be adapted to the past," to an "environment of evolutionary adaptiveness" (Ridley, 2003, p. 191). As Ridley notes, "Inside the skull of a modern city dweller there resides a brain designed for hunting and gathering in small groups on the African savanna. Whatever humanity's mating system was then is what is 'natural' for him now" (p. 189). Humans have been agricultural for less than ten thousand years and have lived primarily in cities for less than one thousand. These are mere ticks on the clock of evolution. For more than one million years before that humans probably lived in small bands and presumably shared the features that are universal among modern humans of all cultures, i.e.,

> A pair bond as an institution in which to rear children, romantic love, jealousy and sexually induced male-male violence, a female preference for men of high status, a male preference for young females, warfare between bands and so on. There was almost certainly a sexual division

of labor between hunting men and gathering women, something unique to people and a few birds of prey. (p. 191)

Before the invention of agriculture, societies that hunted and gathered were mostly monogamous because wealth could not be accumulated. The arrival of agriculture provided the opportunity for some males to be polygamists with a vengeance: "Farming opened the way for one man to grow much more powerful than his peers by accumulating a surplus of food, whether grain or domestic animals, with which to buy the labor of other men." (Ripley, 2003, p. 194). With the development of agriculture and in the highly stratified Oriental societies of early history,

> people seemed to behave exactly as you would expect them to if they knew that their goal on Earth was to leave as many descendents as possible. In other words, men tended to seek polygamy, whereas women strove to marry upward with men of high status.... [M]ating was a trade: male power and resources for female reproductive potential. (p. 197)

Men treated power not as an end in itself but as a means to sexual and reproductive success.

We observe today that humans have developed a system of monogamy mixed with adultery (Ridley, 2003, p. 176). But "[i]t is our usual monogamy, not our occasional polygamy, or adultery, that actually sets us apart from other mammals, including apes" (p. 212). Humans are polygamous or monogamous depending on the circumstances. We have evolved various alternative strategies to achieve our ends. Our heritage evolved us above all else to be adaptable. There are conditions under which philandering is an effective reproductive strategy that might be favored by natural selection and other conditions under which a monogamous strategy is more effective (Dawkins, 1999, p. 10).

Ridley (2003) points out that it is misleading to think that a polygamous human society is a victory for men, while a monogamous one is a victory for women: "A polygamous society represents a victory for one or a few men over all other men. Most men in highly polygamous societies are condemned to celibacy" (p. 180). Infidelity and prostitution are special cases of polygamy in which there are no marriage bonds.

Of course, sex is a source of pleasure as well as conflict although disagreements about sexual availability are probably the most common source of conflicts between men and women (Buss, 2003, p. 144). Conflict erupts whenever the mating goals of one sex interfere with the preferences of the other sex (p. 143). Buss explains that, "conflict per se serves no evolutionary purpose. It is generally not adaptive for individuals to get into conflicts with the opposite sex... [r]ather conflict is more often an undesirable outcome of the fact that people's sexual strategies are different" (p. 143). Buss adds, "Although conflict between the sexes is pervasive, it is not inevitable" (p. 13). "[O]ur ancestors," Buss observes, "[have] evolved psychological mechanisms that alerted them to and helped them solve these [recurrent adaptive] problems. We have inherited from our ancestors these psychological solutions to conflict management" (p. 143).

Negative emotions can be seen as evolved psychological methods to cope with the interference of the achievement of adapted goals (Buss, 2003, p. 143). Although men and women differ in their psychology of mating because they have faced different evolutionary adaptive problems, "mating behavior is enormously flexible and sensitive to social context" (p. 209). Contemporary society, modern technology, the option of abortion, and especially birth control contraception allow people to escape many of the costs of casual sex that burdened our ancestors. Humans now have greater power to design their mating destiny than previous generations ever possessed. This flexible repertoire of mating strategies gives humans significant control over their destinies. Indeed, "Men are not doomed to have affairs because of an insatiable lust for sexual variety. Women are not doomed to scoff at men who are unwilling to make a commitment. We are not conscripted slaves to sex roles dictated by evolution" (p. 209). Human nature is not totally inflexible; it is actually malleable. In the sexual area no behavior is inevitable or genetically preordained. We are not doomed to a single invariant agenda. Evolutionary theory does not say that all human characteristics are hardwired into our genome nor imply "impermeability to environmental influences" (p. 18).

Our evolutionary history has also been responsible for many confluences of interest. Buss (2003) points to the fact that "[m]arital unions are characterized by a complex web of long-term trust and reciprocity that appears to be unparalleled in other species.... Our strategies for cooperation define human nature as much as the capacity for culture or our consciousness" (p. 221). A lifelong alliance of love and monogamous marriage can be considered the pinnacle of human mating strategies.

Although natural selection is random and unpredictable, Miller (2000) asserts that since humans did not evolve solely by natural selection, but also by choosing their sexual partners through language, consciousness, and intelligence, "We are the outcome of [our ancestors'] million-year-long genetic engineering experiment in which their sexual choices did the genetic screening" (p. 10).

Before leaving the subject of the effect of evolutionary factors on human nature and male-female relationships, there are several other elements that should be considered. Ridley (2003) explains that "There is no evidence of genes for different brains, but there is ample evidence of genes for altering brains in response to male hormones" (p. 254). Humans, like all mammals, are naturally female unless masculinized. Male behaviors do not come from specific genes but from the general masculinization of the brain by hormones such as testosterone (p. 112). As such, "the mental differences between men and women are caused by genes that respond to testosterone.... Testosterone masculinizes the body; without it, the body remains female, whatever its genes. It also masculinizes the brain" (p. 254). A man develops a sexual preference for women because testosterone produced by his genetically determined testicles alters the brain inside his mother's womb (p. 264). Testosterone stimulates libido in both males and female, but is the biochemical basis for male sex characteristics. It is the quantity of it that establishes the differences between bodies and brains. At puberty a boy has 20 times as much of it in his blood as a girl of the same age (p. 258).

In addition to the effects of steroids on the development of an organism, it is also known that the maternal environment or reproductive decisions by the mother can have a dramatic effect on the developing phenotype that bias the kind of behaviors seen during the rest of the offspring's life.[1] In addition, there is evidence of symbolic inheritance systems in culture, a genetic evolution of human psychology, which also effect the development of an organism (Jablonka & Lamb, 2006). This has

---

1 Phenotype is the description of the manifest physical properties of the organism including its physiology and behavior.

a Lamarckian flavor, but refers to inheritance of the acquired history and ideas of a culture, not physical characteristics.

It is now believed that there is more to heredity than genes. We can specify four inheritance systems that are responsible for human symbolic functioning as well as gender identity distinctions: 1) Genetically determined anatomy and other genetic pressures, including non-DNA cellular transmission of traits that account for different reproductive roles and sexual strategies; 2) Behavioral factors, especially maternal treatment of offspring that affect their physical and mental development; 3) The learned and interactive contributions of culture, especially the social contract of monogamous marriage; and 4) The development of language and consciousness, which explains psychic structuralization, mental representations, and different psychological imperatives toward core identity and individuation.

Gender distinctions

In this section evolutionary factors will be linked to the development of psychic structure, mental representations, and gender distinctions between men and women. It will be established that evolutionary imperatives, consistent with the fact that females give birth, instill different reproductive and psychic pressures in the developing minds of males and females, forming distinct psychosexual gender distinctions. Freud (1914) and others (Jacobson, 1964; Spitz, 1965; Tähkä, 1987) believe that human life is purely physiological at birth. There is no affective experience because there is no mental capacity. Rather, mentalization develops later with the emergence of a sense of self in relation to an object. Before the accumulation of representation the young infant has no human goal, only the drive to relieve physiological "organismic distress" (Tähkä, 1987, p. 230) or to relieve an imbalance in bioregulation.

Various aspects of early psychic development, including feelings of anxiety, aggression in reaction to frustration, and the development of introjects, can be seen as expressions of adaptation mechanisms, i.e., functions of consciousness. Tähkä (1987) holds that through language and consciousness humans have the "species-specific" ability to develop an experiential world and the unique facility for forming mental representations (p. 242). Structuralization of the mind, with differentiation into self and object representations, psychic introjects, identifications, and other internalizations, is part of the process of ego development.

Tähkä (1987), a drive theorist, states that:

> The use of the first representations as primary regulating structures indicates that the primary motive of the mind is to try to find and ensure gratification by means of... structural elements. While these earliest structures are still directly substitutive for gratification, the proceeding structuralization of the mind, occurring in, and being dependent on, object relations, will create more effective and increasingly complex ways to deal with drive energy, as well as an endlessly ramifying network of secondary motives (cf. Schafer, 1968). (p. 242)

This process of the structuralization of the mind was first proposed by Freud (1915c) and is thought by Tähkä (1987) and others (Loewald, 1971; Schafer, 1968), to be the process that leads to the development of an ego and the formation of conscious functioning and ideational components of mental states. Sandler and Rosenblatt (1962), who state that "self representations... [are] formed by the interaction of... drive, defense, and developing superego functions" (qtd. in Boesky 1983, p. 570), and others (Fairbairn, 1963; Kernberg, 1972; Klein, 1935; Mahler, 1968; Spitz, 1959) take the position that a representational world is a product of ego functions.

Elaborating on Freud's concept of mental representation, Green (1998) explains that "representation is a spectrum that includes the drive, the psychical representation of the drive, the thing presentation or ideational presentation or object presentation, the word presentation and the representation of reality through ideas and judgments related to thinking" (p. 655).

On the other hand, Kernberg differed from Freud's view of the primacy of drives, arguing that "affects rather than drives are the essential motivational force in psychic development" (Boesky, 1983, p. 578). According to Kernberg (1988),

> Libidinal and aggressive drive derivatives... [and] ideational and affective representations of drives are originally undifferentiated from each other and...affect states representing the most primitive manifestations of drives are essential links of self- and object representations from their origin on. I view affects as the primary motivators of behavior. Affects are gradually organized into li-

bidinal and aggressive drives, indissolubly linked to object relations from the onset of individuation. I view self representations and object representations, together with their affective charge, as the building blocks of id, ego, and superego. (p. 319)

According to Schore (2001), "The core of the self is thus nonverbal and unconscious, and it lies in patterns of affect regulation" (p. 37). Other authors who emphasize the significance of affects in psychic development include Bion (1962), Green (1998), Sandler and Sandler (1975), and Spitz (1969). Although Bion agrees with Freud that instincts make an evolutionary contribution and that the most primitive elements of the psyche are linked with sensuous experience, he modified Freud's model of the pleasure-unpleasure principle with the idea that the fantasy of pleasure, the hallucinatory wish fulfillment, cannot occur without the help of an object (see Green, 1998, p. 656). Spitz (1959) emphasized that "emotion plays a leading role in the formation of…the 'organizers of the psyche'…[that serve as] 'emergent dominant centers of integration'" of early ego functions (qtd. in Searles, 1965, p. 523).

Beres and Joseph (1970), distinguishing between mental representation and mental registrations, specify that:

[A mental representation is] a postulated unconscious psychic organization capable of evocation in consciousness as symbol, image, fantasy, thought, affect or action.…When [a] nerve impulse reaches the brain, we assume a registration, which indicates some further process of synthesis or organization characteristic of the organism.…In man the mental registration forms the basis for the development of a mental representation.…[M]ental registrations are transformed into mental representations and, as such, may be evoked as conscious derivatives in the absence of a direct stimulus. (p. 2)

There is a great deal of ambiguity, overlap, and confusion in the usage of representational concepts and structural concepts. Boesky (1983) clarifies some of this confusion by specifying that representational concepts and the tripartite structural model of the psychic apparatus are two separate frames of reference. He points out that mental representations are part of unconscious fantasies, or psychic content, that have emerged from a previously developed mental structure and that organize intrapsychic experience. They are a "precipitate" of subjective personal experiences, not a structure of our minds (p. 581). It is incorrect, he explains, to state that the representation of a fantasy achievement of an unconscious wish "explain[s] the nature of the wish or the method of its transformation" or that representations are transformed into psychic structures (p. 580).

Conceptualizing the mind on the model of a neurologic reflex arc, Freud (1900) assumed that a bodily need produces tension and that the initial function of the mental apparatus is to avoid overstimulation. The simplest way to achieve cessation of excitation is through immediate motor discharge. He proposed that this discharge and decrease in stimulation provides an "experience of satisfaction" (p. 565). Freud hypothesized that the excitation produces a "mnemic image" or a link, "which remains associated…with [the perception and] the memory trace of the excitation produced by the need" (p. 565). After this link has been established, when the need arises again, a psychical impulse will emerge recathecting the mnemic image of the perception and re-evoking the perception, to reestablish the situation of the original satisfaction. "[T]he aim of this first psychical activity was to produce a 'perceptual identity'—a repetition of the perception which was linked with the satisfaction of the need," that is, something perceptually identical with the experience of satisfaction. This impulse is defined as the wish, and "the reappearance of the perception is the fulfillment of the wish" (p. 566). "The first [wish] … [is] a hallucinatory cathecting of the memory of satisfaction" (p. 598). The mind is thus created through a fantasy of pleasure or a hallucinatory wish fulfillment. By relating wishes to an experience of satisfaction, Freud thereby connected psychic representations to bodily needs as an explanation of the formation of the mind.

This formulation places psychoanalysis and Freud's theory of mind within the framework of an evolutionary psychology. In *Freud, Biologist of the Mind*, Sulloway (1983) declares that Freud was the "Darwin of the mind" (p. 239). Parenthetically, Spotnitz (1985) adds to Freud's formulation that if a need is frustrated so that the experience of satisfaction is denied, there is a failure to produce a perceptual identity with consequent frustration that mobilizes rage in the primitive psychic apparatus (pp. 58–59). This pattern reduces tension, but disorganizes the development of the mental apparatus. However, Spotitz believed that aggression in reaction to frustration is an attempt to prevent the formation of a schizophrenic reaction so that this mechanism may actually

enhance the development of introjects and ego differentiation
as part of an evolutionary adaptive mechanism (p. 60).

Taking as an evolutionary fact that a purely perceptive
consciousness is inherent in all animals capable of having
feelings of pleasure and unpleasure, Andrade (2003) delineates a
process in which thoughts are able to take on the same perceptive
capacity as affects and become conscious like them. In his view,
higher consciousness then emerges by acquiring psychic quality
through memory residues of speech (p. 77). He focuses on the
somatic origin of affect to trace the genesis and development
of psychic structure. Agreeing with Freud that affects are
manifestations of instincts, the source being internal physical
excitement derived from basic biological needs, he points out that
Freud interchangeably referred to affects as a sensory concept
as well as an energy concept. To overcome this inconsistency,
Andrade distinguishes between a quantitative factor, a "quota
of affect" (see Freud, 1915b, p. 178), corresponding to the
energy of excitation tending toward discharge and a qualitative
element, affect proper, "corresponding to the perception of the
discharge of the energy, felt as pleasure or unpleasure" (p. 72).
Andrade hypothesizes that "the quota of affect—and not the
affect—occupies (cathects) a memory trace to form an idea
(or representation), which is the *other* psychic representation of
the drive" (p. 73; italics added). The representation or idea is
the memory of the perception of the discharge, whereas the
affect is the perception of the discharge itself. Representation
corresponds to the memory traces of affects (p. 73).

The issue is confounded, however, because representations
from this period of development are assumed to be so intense
that they have characteristics of perception so that the memory
traces may be indistinguishable from the affects themselves. For
this reason, when the quota of affect is increased sufficiently, affects acquire qualities of a perception of a hallucinatory nature.
Even though "the psychic structures were ideational, since they
were memory traces," they also had an affective quality "due to
their strong tendency toward discharge" (Andrade, 2003, p. 73).
Consequently, the hallucination, hypothesized as equivalent to
the fulfillment of a wish, transformed the representation into
affect because it was felt as discharge. The result is a structure
comprised of the juxtaposition of the perception of an affective

discharge with the representation of an earlier satisfaction. According to Andrade, "the germinal core of the mind" develops by means of this primordial operation in which ideational structures develop and branch off from previous affects (p. 75).

Andrade (2003) specifies that "affect is a qualitative concept, sense-perceptive, corresponding to the discharge inside the body of the energy inherent in the quota of affect" (p. 72). The notion of internal discharge is now understood as a consequence of bioregulation mechanisms: "These mechanisms are comprised of neural circuits in the brain coupled to biochemical processes in the rest of the body, the activation of which triggers responses under the form of reflexes, drives, and instincts" (p. 72). Evolutionary pressures impose a process whereby "automatic regulation by the pleasure principle is replaced by thought, at which point ideational structures become superimposed over affective structures....Affect and thought are [then] seen as inextricable" (p. 71). From an evolutionary perspective, adaptive structures generate affective experiences and ideational mental representations, both of which are adaptive processes that motivate human behavior. The ego under the design of the genetic code has structural components and perceptive and experiential components (p. 79).

The scientific evidence supports Darwin's (1859) supposition that human mental capacities arose by natural selection. Although Darwin showed that natural selection occurs at the level of genes, the unresolved evolutionary problem is to show how bodily form, structure, and function—overall morphology and behavior—connect to the micromorphology of the brain since the fundamental basis for all behavior is species morphology (Edelman, 1992, pp. 46–49). Although Edelman asserts that studies in brain biochemistry have made it clear that psychology is grounded in biology, he indicates that further studies will be required to relate "evolutionarily developed brain morphology and circuitry, modulated by biochemistry" to bodily developed morphology in order to find a bridge between psychology and physiology through evolutionary selection processes (p. 40 & p. 107). Spotnitz (1985) emphasizes this point when he notes that "[r]ecognition that transmission across the synapse is mediated by a variety of chemical neurotransmitters...is regarded as one of the most important contributions to neurobiology and knowledge of mental states in this century" (p. 94). Clinical evidence indicates that recognizable loss of specific mental functions occurs when particular brain regions are damaged (Damasio, 1994). These findings support the belief that to understand the evolution of mind we must first understand the basis of morphologic evolution.

The basic biological forces of psychic structuralization and of the formation of self- and object-representations and introjects move each person toward autonomy, i.e., a wish to separate from the mother and from all other objects upon which dependency might develop. However, as Koenigsberg (2008) points out, since autonomy means separation from one's primary source of pleasure, security, and identity, this occurs in relation to a regressive longing to return to symbiosis or a tendency toward fusion and a fear of annihilation because regression to the symbiotic matrix is experienced as death of the self (pp. 25–34). McDougall (2000) also discusses this dilemma:

> [A]ny attempt to disavow the space and the separate existence of the Other gives rise, in the adult-to-be, to an incessant seeking for the illusionary lost fusion....To this eternal quest are added fantasies...and later, anguish in face of the danger of losing the feeling of one's subjective identity...all of which forms an integral part of the psychic world of the infant. (p. 156)

The loss of pleasure as a mentally organizing principle places demands on developing a sense of self that requires integration of conflicting feelings and states of mind.

Since anatomy dictates that females give birth, boys and girls must navigate different adaptive pathways. For psychic coherence, each person must develop a core sexual identity and establish a sense of separate psychic existence. Since males and females have different reproductive aims, they diverge in terms of their reproductive development and their emergent minds. Boys have the task of rejecting the maternal introject to develop a masculine identity. As they individuate, it becomes difficult for them to identify with the mother because of the sexual difference. Boys thus tend to become hostile to or threatened by identification with women. Girls, on the other hand, can more easily identify with and not be threatened by merger with the mother. Girls then strive to feel free of their introjects because they are inclined to stay merged, while boys feel isolated because they tend to reject or disavow a part of themselves, represented

by the engulfing maternal introject. The internalized object
may act as a suffocating weight of oppression to a woman and as
a threat of non-existence to a man. Holmes (2000) hypothesizes
that this is a basic psychological cause of gender differences and
can account for the triangular relationships that characterize
women's psyches and the more dualistic way that men think.

Why is gender identity so difficult to achieve? Every child must
manage to identify itself as either masculine or feminine in order to be in conformity with his or her sense of core sexual identity and must establish a sense of a separate psychic existence.
It can thus be argued that gender differences are created in an
attempt to provide compensation for threats to one's autonomy,
rather than as an assignment of social meaning to biological
differences, reflecting cultural conditions.

Drive theory

Recent findings in neuroscience research establish a connection
between evolutionary theory and psychoanalytic drive theory.
We have traversed the path from instinct to affect by exploring
the relationship between Freud's statements that by instinct "is
meant the somatic process...whose stimulus is represented in
mental life" (1915a, p. 123) and that a wish as "an experience of
satisfaction," produced by fulfilling a need, initiates the development of the mind (1900, p. 565). We have then modified Freud's
formulation with Andrade's observations on the distinction between energy and sensory concepts. How do we get through the
equally tangled path from affect to consciousness?

Andrade (2003) proposes that higher consciousness emerges
by becoming connected to the memory traces of the speech of
objects. Speech, he theorizes,

> depends on action by the musculature of the speaking
> apparatus—that is, since it is a physical process—the thought
> produced by secondary processes [is] eventually able to take on
> the same perceptive capacity as affects and became conscious
> like them....Memory and the reproduction of the object's
> speech [gives] this latter the capacity to be present as an internal
> object, even though it was in fact absent. It [is] then possible to
> transcend concrete symbols of the object because the abstract
> symbols...become sensory by making thought conscious....By
> connecting the ideational structure to reproducible sounds

> to which the object attributed meanings, the association of representations (ideas) [become] sensory—thought [has thus] acquired psychic quality.... [It has become] present symbolically although absent in reality. (p. 77)

In a Darwinian evolutionary path, affective responses are seen as preceding language, followed in turn by primary processes and secondary processes that arise during later evolutionary stages and become integrated into the whole. However, since human affects have broad neural networks, they are both perceptive and conscious and can "pervade thought and its expression" (Andrade, 2003, p. 78). In addition, Freudian thinking implies that while the ego is going through the process of psychic development the function of the self-preservation instincts is supported by the object:

> To the extent that affective structures are...transformed into ideational structures and the primary process is replaced by secondary process, the object is...involved in this passage, not only by affording good affective connections, but also by providing the speech needed for constituting the subject's mind. (p. 79)

This suggests that a good affective maternal-infant relationship will lead to enhanced thought development. The affective environment is the primordial factor in mental structuring and the object and social environment have later roles in the formation of personality (p. 79).

Another view of the emergence of consciousness is presented by the neuroscientist Jaak Panksepp, whose research focuses on emotional systems in the brain. According to Panksepp (1998), circuits for emotions are hardwired, or neurally based, in the limbic system of the brain, which originally developed in mammals millions of years ago. The limbic system communicates with the brainstem, which is the seat of the instincts and is the area concerned with self-preservation and procreation of the species (Shepherd, 2005, p. 48). Emotional potentials exist within the neural circuits independent of external influences. These emotional circuits are "genetically predetermined and designed to respond unconditionally to stimuli arising from major life-challenging circumstances, impelling humans to seek resources to adapt or survive (Panksepp, 1998, p. 48). The search is exciting and the reward is the reduction in tension in the seeking system. "The pleasures and reinforcements of consummatory processes appear to be more closely linked to a reduction of arousal in

[the] brain system," not to some pleasure in consuming as might be assumed (p. 147). As Shepherd (2005) points out, this "represent[s] the ability of certain types of stimuli to access the neural circuitry" and indicates that feelings are generated by, or are the adapted effects of "arousal systems in the brain. They are not causes." "Emotion is an *effect*." (p. 52). This provides a means for an engram for a memory trace to be encoded in neural tissue and for the consequent development of unconscious fantasies and mental representations. "[T]he feeling of wanting, the excitement of going out to search…connects with *a perception* of satisfaction. Every arousal now evokes this perception (or symbol) of satisfaction" (pp. 55–56). A bodily need, which begins as an instinct in the oldest area of the brain, thereby "become[s] symbolized because it provided the satisfaction of tension reduction" (p. 56). According to this argument, evolutionary tension-reduction processes lead to the ability to form mental images and consciousness.

Panksepp's research substantiates Freud's proposal that the mind forms by connecting bodily needs to a psychic representation through a pleasure-inducing wish and lends credence to Freudian drive theory. Freud's theories are also supported by Andrade's thinking. And, as Edelson (1986) states, although not yet established, "[t]he belief that every particular mental state is caused by, or is an expression of some particular physical state…is a tenable common ground upon which neuroscientists and psychoanalysts might meet" (p. 486). He, nevertheless, cautions that neuroscience and the study of mental states as exemplified by psychoanalysis are separate disciplines with their own metapsychology and methodology and cannot be reduced or incorporated into each other.

Edelman (1992), who has conceptualized a comprehensive neural Darwinian theory and model of the development of the brain and the mind based on the basic assumption of mutation due to population gene variance, states that to understand consciousness we must study "structure, function, development, and the evolution of the brain" (p. 68). We must, Edelman adds, have a theory that explains "how the brain areas that emerge in evolution coordinate with each other to yield new functions" (p. 85). He strongly disagrees with the functionalist and objectivist assumptions of some consciousness research, including the computational theory of mind and artificial intelligence, because by relying on principles of physics without resting first on the underlying principles of biology, they do not explicate a biological theory of evolution (p. 15).

Solms (1997) agrees with Freud's (1915b) fundamental position that all mental processes are unconscious and that consciousness is a subjective experience or a quality of mental activity. He states that there is not a cause-and-effect relationship between the brain and consciousness, but that there is a more fundamental process that generates a mental apparatus and a subjective experience simultaneously (Solms, 1997, p. 701). In addition, Solms (2004) writes, "Neuroscientists are finding that their biological descriptions of the brain may fit together best when integrated by psychological theories Freud sketched a century ago" (p. 82). The judgments of Spotnitz, Edelson, Edelman, Solms, and others (e.g., Kandel, 2006) bolster the view that psychoanalysis rests on the foundation of a biological theory of evolution.[2]

Shepherd (2005) explores the issue of how we develop the mental equipment with which to carry on the evolutionary struggle. Integrating the tension-reduction models of Freud and Panksepp, she proposes a connection between evolution and psychoanalysis. Although desire and wish are often used interchangeably, she points out that "desire is closer to lust and the fundamental urge for sex and union" (p. 56). If we replace Freud's use of the word "wish" with the word "desire" or "lust" (or "demand" or "need"), then we can assume that it is procreation that keeps everything going in the evolutionary domain. Language is a bridging property that transforms hardwired tension-reduction circuits in the brain into emotional systems for pleasure and desire. However, Shepherd continues,

> because our world is fraught with dangers, other emotional systems [such as fear, panic, and rage] have evolved which can easily be aroused and interfere with our satisfying desire.... In the animal world, interference with desire results in action of some kind. But in the human world, because of the development of language whereby dangers can be symbolized, civilization, and the cerebral cortex, interfere with desire, resulting in defenses and repetitions. (p. 56)

2 Extensive bibliographies of the problem of consciousness can be found in Edelman (1992, p. 253) and Kandel (2006, p. 453).

These symbols constitute the unconscious positive and negative wishes and fantasies that drive human behavior, and thus human relationships are fundamentally projections of primal fantasies (i.e., transference); that is, human relationships trigger these fantasies.

Archaic images and wishes are products of instinctual drives and therefore products of human evolution. Culture, including, for example, the psychoanalytic treatment method is impacting evolution by, in essence, regulating the primary emotional systems and thereby providing a feedback loop to human instincts, primitive emotions, and gender representations and identifications. Understood from this evolutionary perspective, the mind is a synthesis of affect and thought, both operating in the context of primitive mental representations and fantasies.

An evolutionary model also proposes that the interaction between the structure and functions of the body and the brain leads to a mind and consciousness as an emergent process of the evolution of the human species. Such a neobiological model suggests that Freud was right when he said that anatomy is destiny, but in a different way from what Freud proclaimed. For example, castration anxiety in boys would be better understood as a symbolic fear of succumbing to engulfment, not a dread of being mutilated, and penis envy in girls can be understood as a symbolic expression of a striving for ego-enhancing autonomy, not a sign of narcissism or inferiority. Because boys have to renounce a primary identification in order not to renounce biological urges, while girls do not have to renounce their primary identification in developing a gender identity, there are psychic ramifications: men and women differ in their psychosexual character traits and sensibility about relationships. This contrasts with the contentions put forth by most contemporary, culturally oriented, relational authors who regard sexual orientation, as well as gender, as complex psychological and social constructs, not as extensions of either our anatomically based reproductive capacities or our brain physiology.

An evolutionary view takes the stand that consciousness and the ability to have symbolic mental representations has made humans more flexible and adaptable than our hominid ancestors, leading to the development of culture and civilization. But culture affects sexual reproduction through various forms of interaction so that the process of human psychic development is intimately linked to the process of human cultural development. The mating system of humans, like that of other animals, can be seen as a compromise between the strategies of males and females, and culture and civilization play the balancing role between cooperation and conflict. Monogamous marriage is a social contract that protects the children for the benefit of the species and serves the stability of a culture at the expense of individual needs or preferences. Both men and women have to make sacrifices to the demands of a culture (Tucker, 1993, p. 38).

Summary and conclusions

This paper integrates the recent neurophysiology findings of tension-reduction circuits in the brain, Freudian drive theory, and the evolutionary theory of sexual selection for reproductive advantage to elucidate human gender distinctions. It gives support to the belief that human nature and culture are grounded in biology.

Evolutionary theory proposes that sexual selection for preservation of a species leads to different reproductive roles for each sex—males to produce as many offspring as possible, and females to produce the best offspring possible. Therefore, the genders possess sex drives with separate aims, and they develop different psychological strategies and tactics to achieve them. Thus males and females have evolved divergent psychic content and alternative approaches to relationships.

This biological model of human nature contrasts with the cultural or postmodern constructivist model that the mind is a blank slate, and all behavior is learned through experience or acquired through socialization. This theory implies that heredity can affect the psyche and shape attitudes and behavior as well as affect genes and anatomy. Some evolutionary-oriented psychologists, in fact, attribute an inheritance factor to culture. They posit that due to language and consciousness, the human species has evolved a culture and a biology that continuously interact with and affect each other. Indeed, Robinson, Fernald, and Clayton (2008) point out that

> The genome was once thought to be a relatively passive blue print guiding organismal development. Recent results show

that genomes in fact remain highly responsive throughout life to a variety of stimuli associated with social behavior. Social information can lead to changes in the brain and behavior through effects on the genome. (p. 896)

From the viewpoint of sexual selection theory, because reproductive success is evolution's bottom line, the human mind is understood as a courtship tool that evolved to attract sexual partners, not as a tool that adapted through natural selection solely for individual survival benefits. Due to language and consciousness, and the ability to symbolize instincts, the different reproductive functions of men and women are believed to have led to psychic conflict between the sexes, instead of merely the physical conflict that occurs among other animals. According to Miller (2000), social mores are cultural attempts "to shift male human sexual competitiveness from physical violence to the peaceful accumulation of wealth and status (p. 428). Each sex has evolved ways of acquiring and displaying fitness and social status through various forms of physical, linguistic, intellectual, moral, and economic modes of courtship; and "each human culture has developed its own set of learned fitness indicators" (p. 429).

Sexual selection theory states that when breeding and individual survival come into conflict, breeding takes precedence since reproduction is the essential criterion for the propagation of genes and the continuation of a species. This goal is so central to life in this view that it has influenced the design not only of the body, but also the psyche. Every child must manage to identify itself as either masculine or feminine in order to be in conformity with his sense of core sexual identity and must establish a sense of a separate psychic existence. Dynamic processes that seem to be woven into the evolutionary blueprint, coupled with the fact that females give birth, instill different reproductive and psychic pressures in males and females to achieve psychic autonomy, leading to the emergence of distinct psychosexual gender differences.

Neuroscientific studies indicate that feelings are the adapted effects of the reduction of tension-arousal systems in the brain. Tension-reduction processes in humans are seen as the neural mechanism for the evolution of consciousness and the ability to form mental images. This is in accord with the Freudian drive theory model that human behavior is motivated by feelings, some conscious, some unconscious, reflecting biological instincts.

The concept of the wish suggests a connection between evolution and psychoanalysis. In the Freudian scheme, a bodily need transforms into a wish through an experience of satisfaction from the lowering of a state of arousal. Connecting bodily needs to a psychic representation through a wish is thought to explain where the actual mind, as opposed to the brain, comes from. Tension-reduction processes in the brain are the biological correlate of the concept of the development of a psychic representation through an unconscious wish.

Human relationships, too, are products of primitive mental representations. Since symbols make up the unconscious wishes and fantasies that govern the search for human relationships, relationships are therefore fundamentally projections of primal fantasies. Relationships matter because they trigger these fantasies. These archaic representations and wishes are attributes of the unconscious mental apparatus that are ultimately manifested as the mystery of the experience of subjective consciousness unique to human evolution.

It follows from the evolutionary theory that affective responses are transformed into ideational structures that shape our thinking that as a method of treatment, analytic work, whether adhering to a drive theory model or an object relations view of mental development, will be most effective if it focuses on the transference. The conflict the patient experiences between a tendency to regress to symbiosis and the drive toward autonomy epitomizes the challenge the analyst faces in terms of how to implement a treatment that effectively addresses both emotional dysfunction and rational misperceptions. The treatment approach pioneered by Spotnitz (1985; Spotnitz & Meadow, 1976) and developed by the school of modern psychoanalysis solves this predicament by utilizing empathic and ego-enhancing communications when confronted with preoedipal affective factors and unconscious fantasies and by approaching oedipal-level ideational factors through interpretations. In their view, the transference interventions of the analyst should be made on a demand basis in response to the feelings induced by the patient, taking into account the patient's ego strength and ability to tolerate frustration in an interactive approach that utilizes symbolic and emotional communications and balances the emotional and ideational communications.

references Andrade, V. (2003), Affect, thought and consciousness: the Freudian theory of psychic structuring from an evolutionary perspective. *Neuro-Psychoanalysis*, 5:71–80.

Beres, D. & E. D. Joseph (1970), The concept of mental representations in psychoanalysis. *International Journal of Psychoanalysis*, 51:1–8.

Bion, W. R. (1962), *Learning from Experience*. London: Heinemann.

Boesky, D. (1983), The problem of mental representation in self and object theory. *Psychoanalytic Quarterly*, 52:564–583.

Buss, D. M. (2003), *The Evolution of Desire: Strategies of Human Mating*. New York: Basic Books.

Christakis, N. A. & J. H. Fowler (2009), *Connected*. New York: Little Brown and Company.

Chodorow, N. (1980), Gender relations and differences in psychoanalytic perspective. *Essential Papers on the Psychology of Women*. C. Zanardi, ed. New York: New York University Press.

Cosmides, L. & J. Tooby (1994), Origins of domain specificity: the evolution of functional organization. *Mapping the Mind: Domain Specificity in Cognition and Culture*. L. A. Hirschfeld & S. A. Gelman, eds. Cambridge: Cambridge University Press.

Damasio, A. (1994), *Descartes' Error: Emotion, Reason, and the Human Brain*. New York: Penguin Books.

Darwin, C. (1859), *On the Origin of Species by Means of Natural Selection, or the Preservation of Favoured Races in the Struggle for Life*. London: John Murray.

Dawkins, R. (1999), *The Extended Phenotype*. Oxford: Oxford University Press.

Dobzhansky, T. H. (1937), *Genetics and the Origin of the Species*. New York: Columbia University Press.

Edelman, G. M. (1992), *Bright Air, Brilliant Fire: On the Matter of the Mind*. New York: Basic Books.

Edelson, M. (1986), The convergence of psychoanalysis and neuroscience: illlusion and reality. *Contemporary Psychoanalysis*, 22:479–519.

Fairbairn, W. D. (1963), Synopsis of an object-relations theory of the personality. *International Journal of Psychoanalysis*, 44:224–225.

Fenichel, O. (1945), *The Psychoanalytic Theory of Neurosis*. New York: W. W. Norton.

Fisher, R. A. (1930), *The Genetic Theory of Natural Selection*. Oxford: Clarendon Press.

Freud, S. (1895), Project for a scientific psychology. *Standard Edition*. London: Hogarth Press, 1:283–397.

Freud, S. (1900), The interpretation of dreams. *Standard Edition*. London: Hogarth Press, 4 & 5.

Freud, S. (1912), On the universal tendency to debasement in the sphere of love. *Standard Edition*. London: Hogarth Press, 11:178–190.

Freud, S. (1914), On narcissism: an introduction. *Standard Edition*. London: Hogarth Press, 14:67–102.

Freud, S. (1915a), Instincts and their vicissitudes. *Standard Edition*. London: Hogarth Press, 14:109–140.

Freud, S. (1915b), The unconscious. *Standard Edition*. London: Hogarth Press, 14:168–204.

Freud, S. (1915c), Mourning and melancholia. *Standard Edition*. London: Hogarth Press, 14:243–258.

Freud, S. (1920), Beyond the pleasure principle. *Standard Edition*. London: Hogarth Press, 18:3–64.

Freud, S. (1921), Group psychology and the analysis of the ego. *Standard Edition*. London: Hogarth Press, 18:65–144.

Freud, S. (1925), Some psychical consequences of the anatomical distinction between the sexes. *Standard Edition*. London: Hogarth Press, 19:241–258.

Freud, S. (1926), Inhibitions, symptoms and anxiety. *Standard Edition*. London: Hogarth Press, 20:77–176.

Freud, S. (1937), Analysis terminable and interminable. *Standard Edition*. London: Hogarth Press, 23:209–253.

Gagnon, J. (1991), Commentary on "toward a critical relational theory of gender." *Psychoanalytic Dialogues*, 1:373–376.

Gottfredson, L. (2007), Innovation, fatal accidents, and the evolution of general intelligence. *Integrating the Mind*. M. J. Roberts, ed. New York: Psychology Press.

Green, A. (1998), The primordial mind and the work of the negative. *International Journal of Psychoanalysis*, 79:649–665.

Haldane, J. B. S. (1957), The cost of natural selection. *Journal of Genetics*, 55:511–524.

Hirschfeld, L. A. & S. A. Gelman (1994), *Mapping the Mind: Domain Specificity in Cognition and Culture*. Cambridge: Cambridge University Press.

Holmes, L. (2000), The internal triangle: new theories of female development. *Modern Psychoanalysis*, 25:207–226.

Horney, K. (1937), *The Neurotic Personality of our Time*. New York: Norton.

Jablonka, E. & M. J. Lamb (2006), *Evolution in Four Dimensions*. Cambridge, MA: MIT Press.

Horvath, T. (2000), Our tales are our tails: Miller revives Darwin's "other" dangerous idea. http://cogweb.ucla.edu/Abstracts/Horvath_00.html

Huxley, J. S. (1942), *Evolution: The Modern Synthesis*. London: Allen and Unwin.

Jacobson, E. (1964), *The Self and the Object World*. New York: International Universities Press.

Jaynes, J. (1977), *The Origin of Consciousness and the Breakdown of the Bicameral Mind*. Boston: Houghton Mifflin.

Kandel, E. R. (2006), *In Search of Memory: The Emergence of a New Science of Mind*. New York: W. W. Norton & Company.

Kernberg, O. (1972), Early ego integration and object relations. *Annals of the New York Academy of Sciences*, 193:233–247.

Kernberg, O. (1988), Psychic structure and structural change: an ego psychology-object relations theory viewpoint. *Journal of the American Psychoanalytic Association*, 36S:315–337.

Klein, M. (1935), A Contribution to the Psychogenesis of Manic-Depressive States. *International Journal of Psychoanalysis*, 16:145–174.

Koenigsberg, R. A. (2008), *The Fantasy of Oneness and the Struggle to Separate*. Charlotte, NC: Information Age Publishing.

Laplanche, J. & J. Pontalis (1967), *The Language of Psychoanalysis*. D. Nicholson-Smith, trans. New York: W. W. Norton & Company.

Lieberman, P. (1984), *The Biology and Evolution of Language*. Cambridge, MA: Harvard University Press.

Loewald, H. W. (1971), On motivation and instinct theory. *Psychoanalytic Study of the Child*, 26:91–128.

Lorenz, K. (1966), *Evolution and the Modification of Behavior*. London: Methuen Press.

Mahler, M. S. (1968), *On Human Symbiosis and the Vicissitudes of Individuation*. New York: International Universities Press.

Mayr, E. (1942), *Systematics and the Origin of Species*. New York: Columbia University Press.

McDougall, J. (2000), Sexuality and the neosexual. *Modern Psychoanalysis*, 25:155-166.

Miller, G. (2000), *The Mating Mind*. New York: Doubleday.

Mitchell, S. A. & M. J. Black (1995), *Freud and Beyond: A History of Modern Psychoanalytic Thought*. New York: Basic Books.

Panksepp, J. (1998), *Affective Neuroscience*. Oxford: Oxford University Press.

Pinker, S. (1994), *The Language Instinct: How the Mind Creates Language*. New York: Harper Collins.

Pinker, S. (2003), *The Blank Slate: The Modern Denial of Human Nature*. New York: Penguin Books.

Richardson, R. C. (1996), The prospects for an evolutionary psychology: human language and human reasoning. *Minds and Machines*, 6(4):541–557.

Richerson, P. J. & R. Boyd (2005), *Not by Genes Alone: How Culture Transformed Human Evolution*. Chicago: University of Chicago Press.

Ridley, M. (2003), *The Red Queen: Sex and the Evolution of Human Nature*. New York: Penguin Books.

Ridley, M. (1999), *Genome: The Autobiography of a Species in 23 Chapters*. New York: Harper Collins.

Robinson, G. E., R. D. Fernald & D. F. Clayton (2008), Genes and social behavior. *Science*, 322:896–899.

Sandler, J. & B. Rosenblatt (1962), The concept of the representational world. *Psychoanalytic Study of the Child*, 17:128–145.

Schafer, R. (1968), *Aspects of Internalization*. New York: International Universities Press.

Searles, H. (1965), Phases of patient-therapist interaction in the psychotherapy of chronic schizophrenia. *Collected Papers on Schizophrenia and Related Subjects*. New York: International Universities Press.

Schore, A. N. (2001), The effects of a secure attachment relationship on right brain development, affect regulation and infant mental health. *Infant Mental Health Journal*, 22:7–66.

Shepherd, M. (2005), Toward a psychobiology of desire: drive theory in the time of neuroscience. *Modern Psychoanalysis*, 30:43–59.

Solms, M. (1997), What is consciousness? *Journal of the American Psychoanalytic Association*, 45(3):681–703.

Solms, M. (2004), Freud returns. *Scientific American*, 290(5):82–88.

Spitz, R. A. (1959), *A Genetic Field Theory of Ego Formation*. New York: International Universities Press.

Spitz, R. A. (1965), *The First Year of Life*. New York: International Universities Press.

Spotnitz, H. (1985), *Modern Psychoanalysis of the Schizophrenic Patient: Theory of the Technique.* 2nd ed. New York: Human Sciences Press.

Spotnitz, H. & P. W. Meadow (1976), *Treatment of the Narcissistic Neuroses.* Northvale, NJ: Jason Aronson.

Sulloway, F. J. (1983), *Freud, Biologist of the Mind: Beyond the Psychoanalytic Legend.* New York: Basic Books.

Tähkä, V. (1987), On the early formation of the mind I: differentiation. *The International Journal of Psychoanalysis,* 68:229–250.

Thompson, C. (1990), Cultural pressures in the psychology of women. *Essential Papers on the Psychology of Women.* C. Zanardi, ed. New York: New York University Press.

Tucker, W. (1993), Monogamy and its discontents. *National Review,* 45(19):28–38.

Wikipedia contributors, (2010), Geoffrey Miller (evolutionary psychologist), *Wikipedia, the Free Encyclopedia,* http://en.wikipedia.org/wiki/Geoffrey_Miller_%28evolutionary_psychologist%29

Wright, S. (1932), The roles of mutation, inbreeding, crossbreeding and selection in evolution. *Proceedings of the 6th International Congress of Genetics,* 1:356–366.

30 Fifth Avenue
New York, NY 10011
ebkalin@verizon.net

Women and children first!*

Elisabeth Young-Bruehl

In her consideration of the changing role of women, the author begins by exploring how women have been represented in psychoanalytic thought. She then discusses the development of second- and third-wave feminism and describes the plurality of women's movements that have emerged, worldwide, in the third wave. She closes with some thoughts on how third-wave feminism can inform psychoanalysis.

Over the past 40 years, let us say since 1968, there has been a profound change in the way psychoanalysts, in all schools, have imagined women: who they are, what lines of development are typical of them, what they want, how they live. There has been an effort to leave behind the construction of a representative woman, existing outside of any context, any environment, in order to imagine "women" as a collective, embracing all women in their diversity, in their diverse contexts.

In psychoanalysis there has also been an effort to avoid understanding women on the model of a representative generic man, existing outside of any context, any environment. That is, the idea that a woman is a not-man or a man *manqué* or a deficient, lacking man has been jettisoned. This change has meant that the representative man has begun to disappear, too, although this process is less advanced because thinking in terms of the generic man is still congruent with prevailing patriarchal cultural norms.

Psychoanalysts, like the general public, are still entranced by the question that troubled Freud: "What do women want?" But

*This paper is a modified version of a paper presented at the Center for Modern Psychoanalytic Studies conference, "Sex and the Psyche," New York, December 6, 2008.

most realize at the same time that this question, which implies that someone should step forward with a single solution to the mystery, a single key to its locked door, is really designed to introduce a bold answer that will allay the generalized anxiety disorder of all contemporaries, male and female, who assume that the mystery of what women want is the mystery of why the sexes are so continually at war. Although it retains its allure, the question is now known by many to arise from the wish-laden domain of mythmaking.

A brief history of recent psychoanalytic trends

Before I go on to connect this profound change in psychoanalysis with changes in the larger world, I would first like to track the change historically for it is always illuminating to explore the specific forces and factors that have promoted a change (and inhibited it) and to keep in mind the specific ingredients of change that are still with us and those that were left aside, unexplored, as roads not taken. One of these roads not taken is, it seems to me, especially important for understanding the revisionary road psychoanalysis did take—and the roads it might take.

Even after Freud's 1931 essay "Female Psychology," in which he admitted there were many things he did not know about female psychology and that others—the poets perhaps—might know or would come to know, Freudians quite normally wrote books with "female psychology" in their titles. (Not so many were entitled "male psychology" since that was assumed to be much better mapped territory.) The important collection of papers called *Female Psychology: Contemporary Psychoanalytic Views* (1977) continued the tradition. But in that collection, as in other books of that time, readers could see that the edifice surrounding the answer to Freud's question was collapsing. (Not Freud's own answer, which he had declared inadequate, but the edifice created out of the Freud-inspired speculating and weaving together of psychoanalytic ideas, from the late 1920s reactions to Freud's views up until the early 1970s.) Even though there was still an assumed representative female in this collection of psychoanalytic views, no women of non-heterosexual sexual preference were discussed, no women with histories of trauma, none with minority status based on race or class, nor, for that matter, none with any kind of power, this representative female was not considered in the Freudian manner as not-male. Further, the beginnings of a kind of pluralization were apparent in the questions raised about what constituted normal female development and about whether the concept of normality that had been deployed in Freudian psychoanalysis was inhibiting.

Within a decade, by the 1980s, the traditional psychoanalytic focus on the intrapsychic life and development of "woman" had been completely abandoned by many within psychoanalysis and certainly from every disciplinary direction outside of psychoanalysis where feminists were trying to appreciate the diversity of women's lives and the multiplicity of types of factors influencing them. Not only had the Freudian "female" and Freudian notions of normal female development almost vanished, but methodological questions about how to consider intrapsychic experience in relation to other people (and their psyches), to environments, to relationships, and to observers were everywhere in evidence, a thousand forms of them blooming. Child psychoanalysis was dominated by various kinds of efforts to illuminate "the interpersonal world of the infant," a phrase that still echoed the old habit of abstraction—the "infant," not "infants"—but actually referenced work that was more contextual and relational.

In many ways, the situation was comparable to the one that Freud had faced in the years when he developed psychoanalysis. He had started off with an utterly traditional nineteenth-century medical and psychiatric notion that each disease has a cause, a pathogen, so he had looked for the single cause of hysteria and found it in "precocious sexual experience" (as he announced in the 1896 paper "The Aetiology of Hysteria"). The same cause lay behind obsessional neurosis, he then announced, which allowed him to think that both neuroses share a single cause, so a general causal theory of neurosis was in view. Because Freud also held to the traditional idea that once a pathogen is isolated, the disease can be cured by eliminating the pathogen (and perhaps its carrier), he went after the "precocious sexual experience" in his patients. His technique was to get the patient to talk about her precious sexual experience and its perpetrator and then, didactically, to explain to the patient that this experience was the cause of subsequent distress.

He applied psychoanalytic theory to the wound and awaited an abreaction or a catharsis. When it became apparent to him that neither his assumption of a single cause nor his assumption of a single modality of cure was right, Freud was left confronting a great diversity of phenomena that his over-general assumptions had obscured.

He did not immediately give up the idea of a single cause; he just turned to an alternative one, the Oedipus complex. In "The Interpretation of Dreams" Freud (1900) tried to show that the Oedipus complex and its childhood wishes lie at the bottom of every dream, no matter how diverse the disguising dreamwork and the manifest content of the dream may be. The same, he argued, is true of hysteria with all its multitude of symptoms and conversion symptoms (and one might add from a contemporary perspective, its historical and cultural specificity of manifestation). Similarly, he turned to a new treatment modality. Instead of applying psychoanalytic theory, he waited until the Oedipus complex began to play out—like a current onset of fever—in what he called "the transference," and then he analyzed it there, interpreting (not explaining) the transference, bit by bit, image by image, as he had learned to interpret dreams. Freud had had the insight (which he had struggled toward in the Dora case) that each person's particular way of repeating—indeed, compulsively repeating—her oedipal scenario, or disguising it in dreams, demands a particular interpretative treatment. By the time he focused his attention on narcissism and studied the war neuroses during the First World War, eventually discovering a narcissistic neurosis to make a trio of neuroses, Freud was thinking in terms of a plurality of unconscious oedipal-scenario types: hysterical, obsessional, and narcissistic. These he came to call character types, thereby connecting his work with a long Greco-Roman tradition of character study—the very tradition that the poets who might understand female psychology had inherited. Freud (1916) celebrated this new direction in his work with a series of brilliant essays on "Some Character-Types Commonly Met with in Psycho-Analytic Work" and later in his reflections on the three basic unconsciously determined but environmentally shaped character types in "Civilization and Its Discontents" (1930) and "Libidinal Types" (1931). Despite the continued pull of his hopes for a single cause and single treatment mode, Freud said that each kind of neurosis is "over-determined," that is, it is fed by many springs, and every treatment must steer clear of the kind of single-story suggestibility typical of hypnosis and typical of his own early cathartic and didactic methods. There may be character types, but each person's character is a particular story constructed, as it were, into her or into him as a lived personality.

When psychoanalysts in America and Europe in the late 1970s and early 1980s managed to free themselves to a great degree of the image of "female psychology" and began to confront the diversity of women's experiences, they did not, however, return to take up the unfinished, indeed, still quite unexplored, new direction that Freud had indicated: the direction of plural oedipal stories and characterology. This new direction could have led to consideration of multiple female psychologies and to the conclusion that there is not one universal Oedipus complex with three characterological variants, but a plurality of oedipal variants—just as the anthropologist Malinowski had argued in the 1920s against the rigid, obsessional, and narcissistic opposition of Ernest Jones, a Freudian more Freudian than Freud. Instead, the meeting of feminism and psychoanalysis in the late 1970s focused on the project of freeing women from being thought of psychoanalytically as failed men; it emphasized sexual difference and developmental lines specific to women. It also, generally, focused on the importance of the mother (rather than just the father) in preoedipal and oedipal development of infants and children and on the "reproduction of mothering" (Nancy Chodorow's phrase) in girls.

It seems to me that if the characterological road had been taken decisively, we would have today a psychoanalysis much more richly concerned with the fate of the ego instincts for relationship seeking and ego preservation and ego-ideal formation in various familial and cultural contexts. The traditional Freudian emphasis on sexuality and aggression would have given way to an emphasis on innate sociability and the ego instinctual drive for relatedness. Instead, drive theory—and especially the ego instincts that disappeared into the life instincts and were contrasted to a truly mythic death instinct in 1920—was pushed aside, criticized as insufficiently attentive to object relations as it was in the British object relations tradition and in the feminist appropriation of that tradition. The ego instincts, which are about finding and clinging to objects to satisfy hunger and need for care, protection, and love, disappeared and were not heard of again.

Further, if the characterological road had been taken, I think we would be talking about preoedipal mothering and about the Oedipus complex in various forms as parts of what might be called a "family complex." The Oedipus complex would have come to be understood as a part of the family complex that had been taken or mistaken for the whole, synecdochically, and there would be more attention not just to mothering per se, which is universal, but to its many variants. We would be exploring and cataloging how children internalize from infancy onward family and extended family (cultural) relationships of many sorts, not just the parental ones, and how the whole cluster of any child's internalized vertical (adult-child) and lateral (child-child) relationships, developing from infancy forward, becomes the nucleus of that child's character. The clusteral types are plural for both women and men, but different for men than for women, first and foremost for the reason that the 1970s feminists had emphasized: namely, girls retain their primary relation to their mother as an identification, while most, although not all, boys struggle for disidentification with the mother. Women are also differently related to and identified with other women and men and girls and boys in their nuclear and extended families because they grow up in patriarchy, that is, they grow up "the second sex," dominated, not well educated, constricted in many ways, not accustomed to agency but only to obedience or accommodation or self-sacrifice.

There are many theoretical reasons why this pluralistic characterological road was not taken (or retaken) in the 1970s although some parts of it were, of course, investigated. But the most influential reason, I think, was contextual: psychoanalysts of that period found themselves in the middle of an extraordinary social phenomenon that nearly destroyed psychoanalysis. In that moment of extreme crisis, no one was in the mood to follow a path Freud had pointed to, but that had been little explored by him or by his immediate followers. And, perhaps just as importantly, that crisis left psychoanalysis largely isolated from feminist work that took place outside of psychoanalysis during and after the crisis—a point that I will return to.

The seeds for this crisis were sown by the scientific discovery in the 1960s of physical child abuse (the battered child syndrome), which ushered in a period of discovery of childhood sexual abuse in the late 1970s and early 1980s in America and in Europe. The charge was made that this discovery had been slowed or even blocked because Freud had turned away from his discovery of childhood sexual abuse ("precocious sexual experience") and set psychoanalysis on the wrong road of too much emphasis on the Oedipus complex and oedipal fantasies of sexual seduction. Psychoanalysis was charged with being the great obstacle to the discovery of childhood sexual abuse. The most polemical anti-psychoanalytic book of the period, Masson's (1984) *The Assault on Truth*, actually went further and accused Freud and then all Freudians of duplicitously covering up child sexual abuse in their theories and practices. European and American feminists in great numbers believed this accusation and castigated Freudian psychoanalysis for denying, particularly, father-daughter incest, which child protection services and the emergent international field called "Child Abuse and Neglect" (CAN) were then documenting.

Almost all of institutional psychoanalysis, after some intense resistance to acknowledging the crisis that had arisen, became involved in a collective hand-wringing over Freud's abandonment of the idea that precocious sexual experience was the sole cause of hysteria and obsessional neurosis. The idea that psychoanalysis had taken a fundamentally wrong turn was hardly a spur for reconsidering any features of psychoanalysis's history other than the unhelpful binary that was then set up in a weak effort at reform: attention to intrapsychic life vs. attention to trauma.

No sooner had the reformist idea that psychoanalysis had neglected the study of not just sexual abuse, but trauma in general—including the contemporary traumas related to the Vietnam War that psychiatrists studied and added, in 1980, to the *Diagnostic and Statistical Manual* (American Psychiatric Association, 1980) under the title "Posttraumatic Stress Disorder"—been established than psychoanalysis was attacked from another angle by a motley coalition of critics with quite a different agenda. Their agenda can be summarized under the title of Faludi's (1991) best-selling book of the period: *Backlash: The Undeclared War against American Women*.

In the decade of the 1970s, during which childhood sexual abuse (along with all kinds of violence against women) figured intensely in the American and European public consciousness, psychoanalysis seemed retrograde and obstructionist to all feminists concerned with exposing sexist abuse. To many feminists, the project of a rapprochement between feminism and psychoanalysis in order to revise the Freudian theory of "female psychology" seemed a waste of time since to them it was part of an obsolete, misogynistic science. In the 1980s, as America took a radical political turn toward conservativism and a backlash developed against the feminist emphasis on violence toward women and against the discovery of childhood sexual abuse, psychoanalysis was also labeled part of the problem by conservatives who wanted to attack feminism itself. So psychoanalysis was a target for both feminists and conservatives—a war on two fronts.

The forces of backlash had three major weapons. They said that many accusations of child sexual abuse were false and based on manipulation of children's memories and fantasies by lawyers and therapists, and they even invented a disease, false memory syndrome. Second, they said that many therapists, particularly those specializing in recovered memories, were using Freudian theory to induce their patients to "recover" from repressed abuses that had never happened. Third, they said that the discoverers of sexual abuse were emphasizing abuse in the family and by fathers when the real problem was in community settings like preschools and involved vast conspiracies of pedophiles, including ritual and satanic ritual abusers. Freudian psychoanalysis got implicated in all these charges because it was the theory of childhood fantasy, of repressed memory, and of nuclear family pathology. Ironically, it was tarred by conservatives with the same brush that was used to tar the feminists who had been so critical of Freudianism in the 1970s: Freud and the feminists were anti-traditionalist, anti-moral, and anti-family. Sexual revolution and social degeneracy were the enemies in this socially conservative and religiously fundamentalist backlash.

The backlash in its most extreme form, which had taken the form of moral panic or mass hysteria about predatory pedophiles and satanic ritual abuse, had died down by the mid-1990s, and so-called RMT (Recovered Memory Therapy) was on its way to being definitively discredited, which meant, fortunately, that it was decoupled from its alleged source in Freudian theory. But during this two-decade-long period of the discovery of childhood sexual abuse and then the backlash against that discovery, from approximately 1980 to 2000, the entire theoretical effort from within psychoanalysis to reconsider women—prompted by the earlier fruitful alliance of psychoanalysis and feminist criticism—was under the shadow of the charges and countercharges that came to be known as the "Freud Wars."

Nonetheless, the progress that had been made in reconsidering female psychologies, noted earlier, did not disappear, and several features of it became consolidated conceptually. First, the helpful concept "gender" was assimilated into psychoanalysis from various feminist sources and was used to elaborate more fully than had Freud's term "mental sexual characteristics" all the factors influencing women's (and men's) development that were not biological sexual factors, i.e., not chromosomal sex, hormonal sex, or anatomy and not sexual instinctual drives in their biological aspect. This gender concept aided psychoanalysts in saying there are different ways to become gendered, to come into a particular gender identity. Unfortunately, however, many analysts held on to the idea that there are only two genders: masculine and feminine.

Second, the concept homophobia was articulated at the same time that the American Psychiatric Association depathologized homosexuality, and this move aided psychoanalysts in saying sex and gender development results in different types of sexual object preference—heterosexual, homosexual, bisexual, and fluctuating—each of which is "normal development" (if that concept is used meaningfully, that is to say, if normal development leads to ability to sustain a non-perverse, mature relationship with another whole person). It became less customary to take object preference as the essential element of a person's self and sense of self (the part of identity determining the whole of identity). Third, along with attachment theory, the new field of trauma studies and neuroscientific research on the nature of human memory had given psychoanalysts tools to continue the process of exploring how intrapsychic fantasies and structuration relate to external events. Dissociative states and various kinds of fragmentations of identity became central to psychoanalytic theory and therapy and were applied to the study of women.

Fourth, evolutionary theorists, zoologists, and anthropologists, influenced by changing sexual and social mores, looked out upon the animal kingdom, and especially at the animals evolutionarily closest to human—the chimpanzees and the bonobos—and observed that among these near-kin sexual behavior serves two different and not very compatible purposes in evolutionary terms. It serves reproduction, and for reproduction heterosexual intercourse is required. But it also serves group and subgroup formation and group maintenance, which look very different in the two primate groups because they live under different environmental conditions. All-male subgroups are bonded by the members' homoerotic behaviors, as are all-female subgroups; intergenerational subgroups bond with diverse practices, from grooming to masturbation. Members of a group may find that their erotic attention is divided between their subgroup or groups and the heterosexual male-female reproductive dyad. These observations led evolutionists to understand that among humans, too, the sexual drive ending in reproduction co-exists with other drives or other interests that are just as normal and essential for life and survival. Among these other drives and interests are the ego instincts that I mentioned before, i.e., the sociability and self-preservative instincts.

In the last decade, as the wars and backlashes over feminism and discovery of sexual abuse subsided, psychoanalysts of all schools faced a need for further synthesis of developments in psychoanalysis—many of which took place in the shadows during the Freud Wars decades—and specifically for synthesis of developments in the domain of female psychologies. Although this need is being faced, I think it is also important to consider what is happening now in a wider context—in the wider world—that has not yet, although I think eventually it might, influenced the current synthesizing effort. While psychoanalysts and others in America and Europe concerned with female psychologies were caught up in the huge upheaval that was the discovery of child sexual abuse in America and Europe, a truly monumental shift took place globally. I wonder whether we, as psychoanalysts, can read that shift for its implications about women's developments. What does it tell us about the domain that we are learning to consider, i.e., the interface of unconscious factors and environmental ones.

A changing world of women

Historians agree that there have been two major waves of feminism: the one that arose in the late nineteenth century and crested with the achievement of women's suffrage, starting in New Zealand in 1912 and continuing to the United States in 1919, and the one that arose after the Second World War and reached a decade-long crest between the late 1960s and the late 1970s, before the backlash that I described above. The two periods of rethinking the psychology of women in psychoanalysis coincide with these two waves: the first was in psychoanalysis and was led by women psychoanalysts like Karen Horney; the second was between psychoanalysis and second-wave feminism. In the wider world, there is now a third wave of feminism growing up almost everywhere in the world, and not led by women in North America and Europe. Before asking what it might mean to psychoanalysis, I will describe it through quick sketches, using highly visible events and developments.

The development of third-wave feminism can be charted most simply by looking at the agendas and achievements of the four UN-sponsored World Conferences on Women—the first in Mexico City in 1975, where the UN Decade for Women commenced, the second in Copenhagen in 1980, the third in Nairobi in 1985, and the fourth in Beijing in 1995. A fifth conference has finally been scheduled for 2010 in Sofia, Bulgaria after a difficult backlash period of 15 years. But during the backlash hiatus, the third wave of feminism has continued to gather force, as it has continued to reflect the vision necessary for its emergence—a vision that had begun to be articulated in the Platform for Action that came out of the 1995 Beijing conference. Section 13 of that platform anticipates my description of that vision: "Women's empowerment and their full participation on the basis of equality in all spheres of society, including participation in the decision-making process and access to power, are fundamental for the achievement of equality, development and peace." This statement documents that the women meeting in Beijing assumed that achieving "equality, development and peace" for all humankind, for the species, is now, primarily, women's work, and women, primarily, will bring it about. The message was that in an unequal, unevenly developed, and unpeaceful world no woman would be well advised to wait for the protective call "women and children first!" to come from the patriarchy; women and children must be put first by women, for the sake of all. To use evolutionary terms, women are the subgroup needed for survival.

At Beijing and since then the world has become densely populated with women's groups of all sorts, from the informal to the formally administrated, UN-registered NGOs (non-governmental organizations). (Half of the women-related NGO's now registered at the UN did not exist in 1995.) Groups, circles, solidarities are known to be the momentum, the drive, of the third wave. There is no fear that the organizations will conflict or overlap or fall into a hierarchical arrangement: the more groups the better, the vision says, as the number is heading toward an envisioned tipping point when how women are in groups will be how people are on the planet, when a momentum will become a species change, a new habituation. The theory of change that subtends third-wave feminism is a theory of tipping points reached as the number of women involved in groups and in change increases exponentially. Third-wave feminism is not concerned with women's liberation as a revolutionary project; it is concerned with women's organization or mobilization as an evolutionary project, a change in the species.

All over the world there are action groups like the original suffragette groups; there are consciousness-raising groups like the ones that drove the second-wave women's liberation movement; there are even conversational salons like the protofeminist Enlightenment salons. But there are also groups of every other conceivable kind: groups for rural women, for urban professionals, for students, for women subject to particular oppressions (like lesbians) or particular exploitations (like sex workers). There are groups of young women, middle-aged women, older women; groups for economic development, for saving the environment, for women's and children's rights and legal redress, for political action. There are groups like UNIFEM dedicated to networking and non-hierarchical linking of other groups. Feminist publishing houses and newspapers now exist the world over, as do all kinds of means and media for meeting and exchanging stories and information and projects. A women's rights movement has grown into a leading agenda-setting part of the larger human rights movement, and the force behind a less well-articulated children's rights movement. Tremendous progress has been made in organizing and in achieving declared goals for women and more generally for humankind and the earth and peace on earth.

While this monumental organizing action has been going on, more women than men have been entering the workforce in every region of the world except Africa, and in the workforce they form women's workforce groups. The gap between boys and girls who are being educated has narrowed, and women's illiteracy rates have shrunk in every part of the world, making women more able to organize groups. The average life expectancy of women has increased in developing countries (a sign of improvement in women's health), as the child mortality rate has decreased; and 50 percent of the world's women have access to modern contraception. This progress owes much to the decision of the World Health Organization to prioritize women's health, prenatal care, and children's health. More women are entering into politics, particularly at local levels, and in 25 of the world's nations women make up more than 25 percent of those in national government. Rwanda has become the first state in which women constitute more than 50 percent of its elected representatives. Legislative changes in all regions offer more protection for women's rights, and in many regions liberalization of marriage laws has become an established trend. In most of the countries of the Northern Hemisphere, if not yet the Southern, women are marrying at later ages, or not at all, after attaining an education.[1]

But the counterforce to these signs of progress is all too obvious; you can see it in the way third-wave women have experienced both success and defeat at the UN. For example, on November 21, 2007, the UN General Assembly's draft resolution on the right to food was passed with only one negative vote, from the United States. The resolution protests that each year more than six million children die before reaching the age of five from

---

1 This paragraph is based on the compact world survey in *The No-Nonsense Guide to Women's Rights* (van der Gaag, 2004).

hunger-related illness and that women and girls are disproportionately affected by hunger, food insecurity, and poverty. Girls
are twice as likely as boys to die from malnutrition and prevent-
able childhood diseases, and it is estimated that almost twice as
many women as men suffer from malnutrition. In these statis-
tics the gender discrimination and inequality that are central to
all the world's grave problems stand out clearly—and the worldwide backlash aggravates them. But the resolution itself is testi-
mony to the successful policy strategy of third-wave feminism,
i.e., a strategy of "gender mainstreaming" that makes clear the
role of gender in every grave problem and builds attention to
gender into every proposed solution.

During the period since the 1995 Beijing conference, while
third-wave feminism was gathering force and while, at the same
time, a formidable backlash from threatened patriarchal institutions was resisting it, the gender mainstreaming strategy grew
more and more powerful. Its strength came in part from the
fact that the opposition of "the patriarchy" had become so obvious and was so obviously given its rationale by the fundamentalisms that developed within all the world's major religions.
These fundamentalisms focused on constraining women and
indoctrinating and punishing children. The backlash dictated
that the plight of women and children not be highlighted, not
be prioritized; on the contrary, women and children were to
be even more forcefully kept in their place, within what analysts would call "the oedipal family." To confront the backlash,
particularly in its religious ideological forms with all their regressive consequences, third-wave feminists have had to continuously rethink their own images of women and children. This
meant, ultimately, rethinking their notions of women's agency,
emphasizing how women's agency is in and through relations
with other women. The idea that the way to address sexism and
the centuries-long ignoring of women's rights was to reform
patriarchal institutions and hope for male protection abruptly
receded. A new emphasis on women's groups and institutions
and women as institution-builders came to the fore. In psychological terms, the idea that only women who are male-identified
can be active, can be agents, was understood to be a masculine
idea, a way of keeping women in their place, a way of criticizing
women's initiatives.

It is important to note that this was not a move in the direction of separatism, a strategy that had been advocated in the late 1960s and early 1970s in America and Europe, when radical feminists had argued that, because women would always be second-class citizens in patriarchal institutions, they should withdraw and build their own institutions—from political parties to health clinics to banks. Separatism was never a strategy that could be useful outside of certain specific social strata in America and Europe, and the third-wave strategy that came to the fore in the late 1980s and was articulated in 1995 in Beijing was carefully distinguished from it. No visions of all-women utopias were offered. Facing the worldwide backlash against women, the majority of the internationally networked feminists shifted to considering how women could exercise their agency and build multitudes of institutions that were both sustainable by women and relatively impervious to backlash. The institutions envisioned were not separate from patriarchal, male-dominated institutions; they were connected to them, but on the condition that they not be under their authority or susceptible to being inhibited by them or being dependent upon them. They were set up to be able to grow into leadership organizations on the theory that progressive change builds upon and depends upon change in women's status and power. In every way, it was grasped that images of women as dependent had been the essence of female vulnerability within all kinds of institutions, starting with families. Agency through relations with other women and sustainability became key concepts. And in the domain of child rearing or preparation of the next generation, development from healthy dependency to agency through relations with other women and sustainability became the ideal, especially for girls.

As I noted before, this shift is evident in the statements issuing from the World Women's Conference in 1995 and in the planning for the 2010 conference. But I think that it also shows up clearly—boldly—in the statements of the women who have been awarded the Nobel Peace Prize since 1990—an almost two-decade period in which the prize has been awarded to five women when only six had won it during the prize's entire previous existence. I will also add to the list a man, Muhammad Yunus, who won in 2006, along with his mostly female colleagues in the Grameen Bank. Yunus worked with the same third-wave feminist assumptions that the women who have won the prize share.

Yunus's work dates from before the backlash of the 1980s and resulted in an institution, the Grameen Bank, that was impervious to the backlash. A Bangladeshi economist who earned his doctorate in America, Yunus returned to his country after its liberation war in 1971 and became involved in the national poverty reduction program after the 1974 famine. While he was teaching in Chittagong University, he discovered that the women of a nearby town, Jobra, who made bamboo furniture, were inhibited in the amount of bamboo they could purchase by having to pay for it with high-interest loans. Yunus experimented with making the women small loans at low interest and discovered that they could, with this capitalization, quickly expand their businesses and pull themselves and their families out of poverty. He went on to institute the microcredit business plan by creating the Grameen Bank (the Village Bank), and by 2008 the bank was serving almost ten million small borrowers in Bangladesh. It also sponsored a system of solidarity groups in which the members support each other to secure the loans and make sure that all members are able to pay them back. That is, the women form a group that shares the borrowing risk. The Grameen Bank itself has diversified into units supporting all kinds of ventures, and the model of microfinancing has spread all around the world, including to the United States.

Since its inception, 94 percent of the Grameen Bank's loans have gone to women because Yunus believed that women, who suffer disproportionately from poverty, are more likely than men to use their earnings to support their families and raise and educate their children as well as possible.[2] He realized that in poor women's lives the female solidarity groups were key to the borrowers' sense of belonging and their efforts for a better future. They did not expect support from their husbands, and

2 At about the same time that Yunus set up the Grameen Bank, Allan Rosenfeld, then head of the World Health Organization, shifted the worldwide strategy of that organization toward prioritizing women's health, prenatal care, and early childhood interventions on the theory that a child who gets off to a healthy start in life has much better chance of growing up healthy and able to sustain development and that healthy women would be the best promoters of this understanding.

they certainly did not get it from the Muslim clergy who had, in the 1980s, told women who borrowed from the Grameen Bank that they would be denied a Muslim burial.

Wangari Maathai, who, like Yunus, was born in 1940 and educated in the U.S., founded the Green Belt Movement in her native Kenya in 1977 and came to be known as "The Tree Mother of Africa." In her environmental work, which eventually brought her to found the Mazingira Green Party in Kenya and to work internationally to unite green parties and Young Greens groups, Wangari Maathai always stressed that women were the primary keepers of the environment. The green belt movement employed women as tree planters and farmers, providing many a route out of poverty, and then trained them for political environmental work, turning the cause of environmental activism into a much more general support of women working and taking initiative. Maathai herself paid a direct price for her vision when her husband divorced her, arguing successfully in a Kenyan court that he deserved the divorce because his wife was too difficult to control, too strong. When she protested the judge's concurrence with this complaint, she ended up jailed for contempt. But the movement she inspired and led continued, and she has recently held environmental portfolios in the national government.

To cite one more example: Shirin Ebadi, who in 2003 was the first Muslim woman to win the Nobel Peace Prize, was directly affected by the fundamentalist backlash when she, the first woman to preside over a legislative court in Iran, was demoted to a secretarial position after the 1979 fundamentalist takeover. Unable to practice as a lawyer, she turned her attention to writing about issues that could strengthen the legal status of women and children and to leading campaigns that directly contributed to the large female vote in 1997 that spearheaded the election of the reformer Mohammed Khatami. During the years that followed, she defended people attacked by conservatives within the still theocratic government, and she established two NGO's, the Society for Protecting the Rights of the Child that sponsored legislation against physical abuse of children and the Defenders of Human Rights Center. Both organizations have trained women activists and established links with international organizations that sustain them with funds and pro-tection against attacks from the regime, a strategy that, Ebadi hopes, will make it possible for dissidents to stay in Iran and not join the Iranians in exile. In her autobiography *Iran Awakening*, Ebadi (2006) summarizes her approach to legal and political activism:

> In the last 23 years, from the day I was stripped of my judgeship to the years of doing battle in the revolutionary courts of Tehran, I had repeated one refrain: an interpretation of Islam that is in harmony with equality and democracy is an authentic expression of faith. It is not religion that binds women, but the selective dic-tates of those who wish them cloistered. That belief, along with the conviction that change in Iran must come peacefully and from within, has underpinned my work. (p. 204)

It is in the spirit of third-wave feminism that the recent female Nobel laureates have themselves formed a group, the Nobel Women's Initiative, and that among the activities that they sponsor and participate in is the "Global Call To Action" made by PeaceJam, a group that is working on one of the most wide-reaching—indeed, global—visions of a youth movement ever put forward. PeaceJam organizes working relations between the Nobel laureates and young people from all over the world aimed at initiating "one billion acts of peace," i.e., aimed at reaching a tipping point into peace.

Third-wave feminism and psychoanalysis

Within the International Psychoanalytical Association (IPA), although its membership includes many analysts who would identify themselves as feminists, there is no, or very little, inter-action with third-wave feminism. And the key strategic elements of third-wave feminism—the emphasis on women's institutions and women as institution-builders and the emphasis on prolif-erating and networking women's groups of all sorts and sizes as the momentum of change—are not part of the IPA's own institutions. (Nancy Chodorow has made a historical and socio-logical study of this fact, which is not countermanded by the ex-istence in the IPA of a committee on women and psychoanalysis, COWAP.) Similarly, the third-wave women's experiences are not part of the theorizing about women that appears in its journal or in the regional journals like that of the American Psychoanalytic Association. Third-wave feminism has not had anything like the influence that second-wave feminism had upon psychoanalysis. Neither psychoanalysis as a cluster of institutions nor as a theory, not even as a revised and pluralized theory of female developmental types, has been affected by third-wave feminism.

Interestingly, and not surprisingly, the same could not be said of Jungian psychoanalysis (or analytic psychology), which has its basis in Jung's celebratory ideas about the feminine principle, i.e., which begins from ideas about how women and men differ (although, of course, the feminine principle can be manifest in both sexes). In the Jungian camp, a very active group, or cluster of groups, going under the name Millionth Circle has formed. It is led, or perhaps inspired, by Jean Shinoda Bolen, a medical doctor in San Francisco and a best-selling author, whose first use of Jungian archetypes to talk about women was published in 1984: *Goddesses in Everywoman: Powerful Archetypes in Women's Lives*. This book used seven goddesses of ancient Greek religion to represent different female types:

> These powerful patterns—or archetypes—are responsible for major differences among women. For example, some women need monogamy, marriage or children to feel fulfilled....Such women differ markedly from another type of woman who values her independence as she focuses on achieving goals that are important to her, or from still another type who seeks emotional intensity and new experiences and consequently moves from one relationship or one creative effort to the next. Yet another type of woman seeks solitude. (p. 1)

Jungian psychoanalysis is, basically, a characterology. It traveled on the Freudian characterological road not taken, and so it was well suited to meet the needs of third-wave feminism and to learn from third-wave feminism, particularly about the power potentialities in each character type. Jungian feminism is about agency, and Jungian feminist therapists share Bolen's (1984) belief that, as she has said, "Women seek the help of a therapist in order to learn how to be better protagonists or heroines in their own stories" (p. 1). To use historiographical terms, this therapy is about learning what story (in part told to you by others) you tell yourself and about learning to tell it differently, turning to other women as your hearers and helpers so that at a certain tipping point you become different.

But psychoanalysis does not have to reach for mystical notions of the feminine principle and of inborn archetypes to connect with third-wave feminism or to understand in psychodynamic terms the powerfulness of its theory and practice and what that theory and practice have to teach about how women can be powerful—or how they can be powerful in ways other than those in which the patriarchal narratives, including the original Freudian one, have imagined them to be. In recent years, Freudian-trained psychoanalysts have made a start by turning to the topic of what inhibits women from power or from being powerful. For example, COWAP was one of the sponsors of a February 2000 international conference at Emory University entitled "Women and Power—Psychoanalytic Perspectives on Women in Relationships, Groups, and Hierarchies." The presentations were very illuminating about internal factors—I would call them ingredients or traits of character—inhibiting women. They touched on the following list of factors offered by Chodorow (2002): oedipal guilt; anxiety about separation, loss, or castration; being "wrecked by success" or by spoiling and self-spoiling powers of envy; grandiose narcissistic fantasies that lead to fears of humiliation; conflict about aggression; self-punitive superegos; survivor guilt; and "many other unconscious and conscious fantasies, all of these put together differently by different individuals" (p. 18). But the question, where do powerful women get their power? was hard to ask in this context of concern with inhibitions developed in and fostered by sexist societies. Within third-wave feminist groups, the answer to the question is simple: from other women who, as is so clear in the Grameen Bank example, share the risk of investing in a better future, and a better story for women and children.

Conclusion

In closing, I want to offer a way to translate this simple, powerful "sisterhood is powerful" declaration into psychoanalytic terms. What is it that women can give each other in groups? The experience of *power*, which can be simply defined in terms that are both psychoanalytic and political as acting together with equals. If a women's group is non-hierarchical and non-prescriptive, truly a group of equals, it operates like a therapeutic situation, that is, it is aimed toward constantly revising the story (with many variants) of necessary submission and accommodation and self-sacrifice that women everywhere learn to tell themselves. The revision process requires safety and trust to promote openness and revelation of self, revelation of who you are. As a forum, the group operates as an expression of shared experience or healthy narcissistic transference. It allows all its members the experience of being understood, of experiencing from other members the sense that: "I have also been through something similar though not the same as what you are talking about." The group can build on experiences of similarity and communality, not upon difference since the differences among women are differences of character type, not of sexually based mastery or rulership rooted in child-parent psychodynamics. Ruling over is the opposite of acting together.

A women's group can aim toward action that reflects the biologically given female capacity for reproduction, which is family-group generation capacity and more generally a capacity for nurturance and generativity. The group aims to establish this capacity in the world outside of the home, augmenting the family circle by connecting it to other circles as its members act together. Power makes power. This is why third-wave theorizing places such stress on increasing participation and on tipping points of power. Men can have the experience of acting together as equals, but they cannot by virtue of their biology have the further experience of gestating future generations, future circles, of that acting-together experience. Thus their groups are always degenerating into groups of rulers and ruled, fathers and sons beset by succession crises or questions about how the group will be sustainable as the king grows old. The women's group is inherently future-oriented, that is, it is for the women in it and for their children and grandchildren and the children they take responsibility for. They are not tied to the past or, as men are, to the status quo of patriarchal privilege because their experience of the past is that it enchains them, and they know that ultimately they have nothing to lose but their chains. This orientation to the future and to sustainability means that the group is not distracted from power augmentation and extension by a resort to violence or by the illusion, typically masculine, that using violence brings power. As Gandhi understood, women's groups are inherently non-violent, and it is this that gives them the possibility of containing and channeling women's aggression rather than turning violent or self-destructive.[3] The model or group-ideal (like a collective ego-ideal) of a women's power group is a female sibling group in which everyone grows up to be equal in opportunity and reward. It is not dominated by either fathers or mothers, in reality or internally, who view themselves as rulers or critics or dispensers of rewards. The mothers invoked in third-wave feminist visions, the ancestral mothers, are idealized mothers, wished-for mothers: generative toward the group members as the group members wish to be toward each other and their children. Not all women's groups, of course, live up to the possibilities that I have described—but they do have these possibilities!

references   American Psychiatric Association (1980), *Diagnostic and Statistical Manual of Mental Disorders*. 3rd ed. Washington, DC: American Psychiatric Association.

Blum, H., ed. (1977), *Female Psychology: Contemporary Psychoanalytic Views.* New York: International Universities Press.

Bolen, J. S. (1984), *Goddesses in Everywoman: Powerful Archetypes in Women's Lives.* New York: HarperCollins.

Chodorow, N. (2002), Glass ceilings, sticky floors, and concrete walls: internal and external barriers to women's work and achievement. *Constructing and Deconstructing Woman's Power.* B. J. Seelig, R. A. Paul, & C. B. Levy, eds. London: Karnac.

Ebadi, S. (2006), *Iran Awakening.* New York: Random House.

Faludi, S. (1991) *Backlash: The Undeclared War Against American Women.* New York: Crown.

Freud, S. (1896), The aetiology of hysteria. *Standard Edition.* London: Hogarth Press, 3:187–221.

Freud, S. (1900), The interpretation of dreams. *Standard Edition.* London: Hogarth Press, 4 & 5.

Freud, S. (1916), Some character types met with in psychoanalytic work. *Standard Edition.* London: Hogarth Press, 14:309–333.

3 Gandhi said, "If nonviolence is the law of our being, the future is with woman." See Usha Thakkar's (2002) essay, "Breaking the Shackles: Gandhi's Views on Women."

74

Freud, S. (1930), Civilization and its discontents. *Standard Edition.* London: Hogarth Press, 21:59–145.

Freud, S. (1931), Libidinal types. *Standard Edition.* London: Hogarth Press, 21:215–220.

Freud, S. (1931), Female psychology. *Standard Edition.* London: Hogarth Press, 21:223–243.

Masson, J. M. (1984), *The Assault on Truth: Freud's Suppression of the Seduction Theory.* New York: Harper Perennial.

Platform for Action, section 13 (1995), Fourth World Conference on Women, Beijing Declaration. www.un.org/womenwatch/daw/beijing/platform/declar.htm

Thakkar, U. (2002), Breaking the shackles: Gandhi's Views on Women. *Meditations on Gandhi: A Ravindra Varma festschrift.* M. P. Mathai, M. S. John, & S. K. Joseph, eds. New Delhi: Concept Publishing Co.

van der Gaag, N. (2004), *The No Nonsense Guide to Women's Rights.* Toronto: New Internationalist Publications.

229 Major Street
Toronto, ON M5S 2L5, Canada
youngbruehl@gmail.com

What do postmodern feminists want from Freud and psychoanalysis?*

Siamak Movahedi

Commenting on Young-Bruehl's exposition of the complex subject of gender and psychoanalysis, the author examines the ways that third-wave feminism has informed the evolving nature of psychoanalytic theory and its influence on the Freudian inheritance in particular. He suggests that psychoanalysis, like feminism and other theoretical modalities, are discourses, and he considers their relations and agendas in a social context.

Young-Bruehl (2008) argues that "in an unequal, unevenly developed, and unpeaceful world no woman would be well advised to wait for the protective call 'women and children first!' to come from the patriarchy; women and children must be put first by women, for the sake of all" (p. 64). This is the third-wave feminist position that has been slow to infiltrate psychoanalytic thinking. Yet to Young-Bruehl, psychoanalysis has gone through a profound change since Freud's time. Psychoanalysis no longer searches for a typical woman, a representative case of femininity, to help unravel the enigma of woman's desire. The representative woman has begun to disappear along with the notion of the representative man although the idea of the generic man shows much more resistance to dropping out of the patriarchal *Weltanschauung*.

I agree with much of Young-Bruehl's discussion of this complex subject although at times she sounds more like a second-wave

*This paper is a modified version of a paper presented at the Center for Modern Psychoanalytic Studies conference, "Sex and the Psyche," New York, December 6, 2008.

rather than a third-wave feminist. Third-wave feminism is a postmodern and poststructural discourse that assumes an inherent ambiguity in the language and categories of gender. What is a woman and what is a man are as problematic questions as what is feminine and what is masculine. The postmodern thinkers question the credibility of the second-wave feminists' grand narrative of patriarchy and victimization.[1] They also challenge the second wave's essentialist definitions of femininity as exemplified in the lives of upper-middle-class white women. Anatomy is not destiny although one cannot ignore the significance of the materiality of the body. When it comes to masculinity, femininity, beauty, and other sexual signifying symbols, the body is itself social though sexual desires cannot always be located in the desire of the Other, unless by the "Other" we mean the human species. The third-wave feminists depart from their mothers' ideological movement in that they continue to fight for equal rights, but not to the detriment of their sexuality. Like the characters in *Sex and the City*, they find the girly culture, the lipstick, and the sex and pleasure to be empowering (Baumgardner & Richards, 2000; Straus, 2000). For them anatomy is not a ticket to manhood or womanhood. Many third-wave feminists voted for Barack Obama rather than for Hilary Clinton. They saw no ideological contradictions or false gender consciousness in voting for a man rather than for a woman. Some of them were quite unabashed in saying that Hilary Clinton was not a woman. However, feminist movements and psychoanalytic theories may change or go through revisions without departing significantly from the dominant symbolic order.

In discussing sex and gender in a sociology class recently, I asked the students: if they could temporarily be the other gender, who among them would like to be so and for how long? Out of 100 students, 15 raised hands; they were all women. Not even a single man raised his hand. I am sure many of them were silently entertaining the fantasy of temporarily being a woman, but they could not dare to publicly announce it. Many of them wouldn't even dare to allow that fantasy to visit their consciousness. My question seemed to make a group of student hockey players who always sit together in the back of

1 See Lyotard (1984) for a discussion of modern and postmodern conditions.

the class particularly anxious. They moved closer to one another almost sitting in one another's lap, giggling nervously,
and whispering to each other. They looked pathetically weak
and vulnerable.

Why do we need to resort to the phallus to explain the role-
imprisonment of these students—both men and women? The
process of gender identity and of modeling oneself after another
person is quite complex. We are born within—not with—an in-
tricate system of symbolic codes that dictate what imaginary or
real person in our lives we are allowed to emulate. The simple
notion of an anatomically structured set of identifications is too
inadequate as an explanatory tool.

The journalist Norah Vincent (2006) went undercover in the
world of men to study how it felt to be a man. Talking about her
fears in playing the role of a man, she writes:

> It wasn't being found out as a woman that I was really worried
> about. It was being found out as less than a real man, and I sus-
> pect that this is something a lot of men endure their whole lives,
> this constant scrutiny and self-scrutiny. Somebody is always evalu-
> ating your manhood, whether it's other men, other women, even
> children. And everybody is always on the lookout for your weak-
> ness or your inadequacy, as if it's some kind of plague they're ter-
> rified of catching, or, more importantly, of other men catching. If
> you don't make the right move, put your eyes in the right place at
> any given moment, in the eyes of the culture at large that threat-
> ens the whole structure. Consequently, somebody has always got
> to be there kicking you under the table, redirecting, making or
> keeping you a real man, and that, I learned very quickly, is the
> straightjacket of the male role, and one that is no less constrictive
> than its female counterpart. You're not allowed to be a complete
> human being. (p. 276).

> Boys have sensitivity routinely mocked and shamed and beaten
> out of them, and the treatment leaves scars for life. Yet we women
> wonder why, as men, they do not respond to us with more feel-
> ings. (p. 286)

The metanarrative of the second-wave feminists clearly defined
the vulnerable characters in Vincent's story as the Other, the
enemy. We, i.e., men, were the enemy. As long as they had their
sisters, or using Young-Bruehl's language, their "siblings" whose
groups are "inherently" different from men's groups, they had
no use for us.

So where does Young-Bruehl's position fall in this spectrum? Young-Bruehl's (2008) paper is really two papers. The first part is a psychoanalytic paper, and the second part is a sociological paper. The bridge between the two remains ambiguous. I have no contention with her criticism of Freud's theory of female sexuality and no disagreement with her description of women's increasing achievements or her articulation of the third-wave feminist's global program. I just don't know what she expects in retrospect from Freud or from contemporary psychoanalysis. I do not believe that her intention here is to offer a feminist critique of Freud's theory of female sexuality. Such a critique is not something new or original. So, What does Dr. Young-Bruehl want?

To get a better understanding of her position, I looked at a few of her papers on gender and psychoanalysis and at her book *Freud on Women* (Young-Bruehl, 1990). In this book, Young-Bruehl, commenting on the focus of feminists' criticism of Freud, writes:

> Although many specific dimensions of Freud's very complex and many-times revised presentation of female psychology have been criticized, it is no exaggeration to say that behind every specific criticism looms one large objection. Freud, so this objection goes, viewed femininity as failed masculinity. His claim that the libido is not just active but masculine has correlatives in every facet of his theory.... This general criticism has been highlighted by feminists for two quite different purposes. On the one hand, the fact that psychoanalytic theory is obviously not an equal-opportunity theory has meant for some that it should be rejected or radically cleansed of its bias against women. On the other hand, the psychoanalytic portrait of the female as a failed male has been accepted as the deepest analysis available of the effects of patriarchy...on men's attitudes toward women and women's attitudes toward themselves. *Here it is not the view that is objected to, but the reality which the view reflects, the reality that must be addressed by any truly radical social reform.* (p. 41; italics added)

From this it follows that if the social structural reality of women's lives, opportunities, and rights are changed, psychoanalytic theories or concepts should or would follow. This is a postmodern and poststructural position. It is the position of sociology of knowledge, originally advanced by Karl Marx and later by Karl Mannheim (1968, 1998), that searched for the content and evaluative criteria of scientific theories in social structure.[2] Here, if we apply Marx, Manheim, and Freud himself to the text of Freud's theories, we can reconstruct a picture of his psyche and the social reality within which it was embedded. Psychoanalysis itself is a sociocultural construct. It is an attempt to re-present another social construct—mind or psyche—from a subject's ideological position. There is no direct and unmediated access to the reality of sex or psyche.

Looking at the situation of women in Germany or in the world during the late nineteenth and early twentieth centuries, Freud (1905, 1920, 1931) equated femininity with passivity and masochism. His theory mirrored the social reality of the time (Makari, 1991). Yet he was aware on some level that what he was observing had been partly imposed on women by society. We may even argue that inhabiting the language and culture of Germany at the time, the language spoke him. (Of course, his personal unconscious also spoke him—if one can make a distinction between personal and social unconscious.) Although the binary oppositions of presence/absence, masculine/feminine, and active/passive structured his thinking on gender in terms of the penis, he exhibited a great deal of tension in this construction. In fact, one may argue that he tried to do Derrida's job of deconstructing gender by showing that the two sexes would collapse into one another and that there was no such thing as pure heterosexuality or homosexuality. At times Freud impresses us as coming close to the discovery of gender as different from sex, but then, becoming overwhelmed with the social reality of the time, he resorts to pseudoscientific language of anatomy to make sense of cultural constructs.[3] He finds "only one libido, which serves both the masculine and the feminine sexual functions. To it itself we cannot assign any sex." But then

2 I have personally argued for this position as early as 1976 in a published paper on the sociology of science (Movahedi, 1976).

3 "I surmise that the insistence on affiliating ourselves with the so-called 'natural sciences,' viz., biology, neurobiology, chemistry and physics, may represent a quest for professional respectability rather than a quest for scientific 'truth.' That is, this whole controversy might be considered a problem in the sociology and politics of science rather than one of theory, methodology or epistemology. Here, I rephrase Rorty's (1979, 1992) suggestion that given the prestige of the physical sciences, the persistence over the explication of the symbolic action in terms of biology or neurophysiology may be a reflection of 'physics envy,' an analogue of the 'penis envy' complex" (Movahedi, 1996, p. 28).

he admits that, "following the conventional equation of activity and masculinity, we are inclined to describe it as masculine" (Freud, 1933, p. 130). He does not elaborate, however, on why he follows this conventional equation in his so-called "scientific theorizing on the psychology of women." Yet, he does admit that he does not "lay claim to more than an average validity" in his assertions on the psychology of women and reminds us that "it [is not] always easy to distinguish what should be ascribed to the influence of the sexual function and what to social breeding" (p. 132).

Meltzer (1999) in his paper "Literature, Psychoanalysis and Gender" begins his discussion asking how and "why, psychoanalysis keeps returning like a kind of constant itch to the feminist project in the West" (p. 361). He then argues that while Freud's papers were written within a clinical context, the critics interrogate the text for epistemological reasons including the notion of gender constructs. As such, he states, "the Freud of theory is disjuncted from active clinical praxis. Freudian thought in the works of what we might also call postmodernism is one that a clinical psychologist or psychiatrist, or indeed analyst, will barely recognize" (p. 361). Although I do not completely agree with Meltzer's distinction between interrogating a text and engaging a clinical narrative, I know that in the analytic situation most analysts have little use for much of the metapsychological theories of classical psychoanalysis. The notion of lack or the question of the masculine or feminine nature of libido is a part of the numerous metaphysical assumptions that psychoanalysis can do without.

However, Young-Bruehl's concern in her paper is not with the metapsychological, clinical, or scientific status of psychoanalysis. She is concerned with the social reality that hosts our theories. In the realm of social reality, it is the belief or fantasy that structures the nature of human relationship. Of course if Young-Bruehl were a Marxist, she would argue the opposite, i.e. that it is the structure of human relationships that forms beliefs or fantasies. And in either case, metaphysical assumptions and pseudoscientific explanations are at times much more potent determinants of people's thoughts, feelings, and action than scientific theories. A good example is the creationist or the so-called intelligent-design charade. According to a 2004 Gallup poll, 45 percent of

Americans still believe that God created humans without evolution ever taking place. Apparently all the scientific developments in physics, chemistry, and biology have had little impact on the belief structure of half of the population. In a similar vein, in the cultural domain it matters little whether there is any scientific basis to the distinction between the constructs of sex and gender. People's cultural beliefs inform their views about sexuality and gender. According to W. I. Thomas (1966), one of the last century's most prominent sociologists, "If people define situations as real, they are real in their consequences" (p. 301). That is, what matters is people's definition of situations rather than any facts. By the way, it is here that sociology and psychoanalysis meet. Freud, as with most contemporary analysts, is concerned not with the "real" situation, but rather with the individual's interpretation of it. The patient's belief or fantasy about the experience of a sexual seduction has a greater impact than the objective fact of seduction itself. If one defines a seduction fantasy as real, it will become real in its consequences. Along the same line, what changes people's social reality and their definitions of situations is an emotionally evocative event rather than rational interpretation, explanation, or clarification.

It is ironical that the day after Obama's election, I was scheduled to give a talk on race relations. It suddenly dawned on me that I had to rewrite my whole talk. The election of Barack Obama had altered the discourse on race in the United States. Although every ideological group invokes its own narrative to explain the election of Obama, the change in people's social reality and in their system of beliefs is just about to begin. A *black* family in the *White* House is going to fundamentally destabilize the white-black binary opposition. A black family in the White House is going to leave a permanent imprint on the American soul—you may even say on the global soul. This election has changed the paradigm and the discourse on race. Even David Duke will soon find his old racist discourse quite obsolete. The same thing is true with sex and gender. The new discourse on gender, brought about through the struggle of women's movements and also through social, political, and economic changes, has and will continue to render unusable the old misogynous conceptualizations. Frankly, my recent re-reading of some of the early psychoanalytic papers on sexuality made me cringe.

Much of it felt ego-dystonic. That would be the case if we were to examine the history of most fields of endeavor in human sciences. In fact, if we were to put Freud in the analyst's chair, he would be quick to get us to see that the grounds on which theories stand are paved with uncertainty and that the reality they represent is suspect. The past is a reconstruction, the memory is a perception, and the perception is a fantasy. This is the image of "de-centered" knowledge. Deconstruction of our illusions of immutable truth is one of the goals of psychoanalysis.

references   Baumgardner, J. & A. Richards (2000), *Manifesta: Young Women, Feminism, and the Future.* New York: Farrar, Strauss & Giroux.

Freud, S. (1905), Three essays on the theory of sexuality. *Standard Edition.* London: Hogarth Press, 7:125–245.

Freud, S. (1920), The psychogenesis of a case of homosexuality in a woman. *Standard Edition.* London: Hogarth Press, 18:145–172.

Freud, S. (1925), Some psychical consequences of the anatomical distinction between the sexes. *Standard Edition.* London: Hogarth Press, 19:241–258.

Freud, S. (1931), Female sexuality. *Standard Edition.* London: Hogarth Press, 21:221–244.

Freud, S. (1933), New introductory lectures on psychoanalysis. *Standard Edition.* London Hogarth Press, 22:1–182.

Makari, G. J. (1991), German philosophy, Freud, and the riddle of the woman. *Journal of the American Psychoanalytic Association,* 39:183–213.

Lyotard, J. (1984), *The Postmodern Condition: A Report on Knowledge.* G. Bennington & B. Massumi, trans. Minneapolis: University of Minnesota Press.

Mannheim, K. (1968), *Ideology and Utopia: An Introduction to the Sociology of Knowledge.* L. Wirth & E. Shills, trans. New York: Harcourt, Brace & World.

Mannheim, K. (1998), *Essays on the Sociology of Knowledge: Karl Mannheim: Collected English Writings.* Vol. 5 of *Routledge Classics in Sociology.* New York: Routledge.

Meltzer, F. (1999), Literature, psychoanalysis, and gender. *The Annual of Psychoanalysis,* 26:361–370.

Movahedi, S. (1976), Methodological schizophrenia: a problem in the sociology of science. *International Journal of Contemporary Sociology,* 13:81–92.

Movahedi, S. (1996), On cause, teleology and the question of drive versus wish: a comment on Nigel Mackay's refutation of purposive explanations. *Modern Psychoanalysis*, 21:19–29.

Rorty, R. (1979), *Philosophy and the Mirror of Nature*. Princeton: Princeton University Press.

Rorty, R. (1992), Historical truth and narrative truth. Invited symposium, twelfth annual spring meeting of the American Psychological Association, Division of Psychoanalysis, Philadelphia.

Straus, T. (2000), A manifesto for third-wave feminism. http://www.alternet.org/story/9986.

Thomas, W. I. (1966), The relation of research to social process. *W. I. Thomas on Social Organization and Social Personality*. M. Janowitz, ed. Chicago: University of Chicago Press.

Young-Bruehl, E. (1990), *Freud on Women*. New York: W. W. Norton.

Young-Bruehl, E. (1996), Gender and psychoanalysis. *Gender and Psychoanalysis*, 1:7–18.

Young-Bruehl, E. (2008), Women and children first! *Modern Psychoanalysis*, 34:53–75.

Vincent, N. (2006), *Self-Made Man*. New York: Viking Press.

252 Waban Ave
Newton, MA 02468
siamak.movahedi@umb.edu

The perilous umm: a note on the contact function and a countertransference resistance*

Mary Shepherd

This paper explores causes and manifestations of a particular countertransference resistance and suggests how the patient's contact functioning can be used to understand and to resolve primitive character repetitions.

> In the middle of nowhere life inexorably calls to life.
>
> Stanley Kunitz, "The Flight of Apollo"

The patient enters the office, takes the couch, and begins to talk. After five or ten minutes he pauses; the analyst says, "Umm" and the patient goes on talking. This pattern continues for the hour. The analyst may say a few words at the end. The patient leaves. What was going on here? What was the meaning of the umm? The patient wanted the analyst to umm and the analyst ummed. The patient, like most people, didn't want to ask for anything. He wanted the analyst to know what he wanted. The analyst knew. The umm means, "I'm here. I'm listening." The umm is "Yes, I know what you are talking about." Umm is "I agree with you. I remember what you were talking about last week. I under-stand you." Umm is the all-knowing preoedipal mother meeting

---

*An abbreviated version of this paper was presented at the annual meeting of the Vermont Society of Modern Psychoanalysis, Brattleboro, VT, March 7, 2009.

all your needs. Umm is delicious, unconditional oneness. Umm is ecstasy.

What could be wrong with this? The problem is that the umm is unsolicited; it is not a response to a direct request by the patient. Even though the patient may appear to be looking for a response, the analyst has reacted without being verbally asked to do so. Consequently, the analyst introduced herself as a separate, all-knowing object into the fragile psychic structure of the patient. This is dangerous. It is arbitrary gratification that has the potential to increase the patient's craving for perfect understanding—a craving that everyone has—and thereby to infantilize him. Even more importantly, umming mollifies the patient and keeps him from knowing and revealing his fundamental patterns of relating to an object and from trying to get his needs met. Similarly, the analyst loses the opportunity to study those patterns that constitute the basic, hard-wired character defenses, the repetitive patterns that keep the patient from having a satisfying life. It is these repetitions that are the most difficult to reach and to resolve, but whose resolution is critical to the essence of a curative analysis. Umming, then, is a countertransference resistance that can be the insidious destroyer of an analysis.

The contact function

The contact function, the way in which the patient tries to contact the analyst, is a "royal road" to understanding unconscious functioning. It is a multi-layered and multidimensional concept. It is both a resistance to talking and a crucial indicator of relatedness. Deceptively simple on the surface, it can lead the analyst to the deepest levels of conflict in the patient. On a conscious level it means simply the patient's "verbal attempts to gratify an immediate need for words from the analyst" (Spotnitz, 1985, p. 154). It almost invariably indicates the presence of a resistance, resistance being defined as whatever interferes with verbalizing associations, thoughts, feelings, and memories in a progressive manner. Spotnitz advocates reflecting the patient's verbal attempt at contact in order to provide "in essence, brief verbal feedings on a self demand schedule" and therefore to "minimize the amount of frustration-tension to which the patient is exposed while lying on the couch . . ." (p. 155). The immediate goal is to help the patient go on talking. But more importantly, in addition to expressing an immediate need for some form of gratification, Spotnitz says that the patient's contact function "might be equated with the 'infant's struggling attempt to make contact with the distant, preoccupied mother, a kind of loss known at times to us all' (Oremland, 1980, p. 311)" (qtd. in Spotnitz, 1985, p. 154). The early object was not there, not in the right place at the right time. In other words, the attempt to contact the analyst reveals the way the patient dealt with frustration in his earliest object interchanges. In his contact or lack of contact with the analyst, he is repeating behavior resulting from these early failures in maturational interchanges, and his behavior is laden with information about early frustration and defenses.

Psychological reflection of the patient's contact means that the analyst does not answer a question or provide advice, but finds a moderately gratifying way to repeat the question to the patient. Again, the goal is to gratify an immediate need for words but at the same time to maintain enough frustration so that "*the patient's customary patterns of dealing with a frustrating object are activated*" (Spotnitz, 1985, p. 155; italics added). As the transference develops, these defenses become highly emotionally charged. And as the analyst reflects the contacts, the patient will not be exposed to an inordinate amount of frustration, yet will reveal to the analyst his earliest defensive pathways. Resolution of these repetitions is central to a successful analysis.

The contact function of the patient is a concept described by Spotnitz as early as 1956. He had spent many years researching schizophrenia and gradually came to the conclusion that psychoanalysis had the potential to reverse this condition. Central to his discoveries was the concept of the contact function. Schizophrenics, he observed, are basically out of contact with people. They were defending themselves against powerful aggressive forces. Their libido is focused on inhibiting their aggression, rather than on relating to others. They cannot be reached by kindness or reason. Spotnitz recommends studying and reinforcing their fundamental ways, both symbolic and emotional, of attempting contact until they gradually become comfortable enough to venture out. For example, he sat silently with a catatonic patient for two years, making only the same physical moves the patient made. Finally the patient spoke. He also reflected the affect and behavior of an angry, demanding patient, who ordered, "Get me some cigarettes!" Spotnitz responded, "Why should I get you some cigarettes?" This work, at primitive levels of psychic formation, clearly revealed basic conflict dynamics. The contact function was a window on the fundamental levels of functioning that exist in all of us.

The repetition compulsion

Spotnitz based his exploration of effective technique on Freud's drive theory. This maturational, biologically based theory conceives of the individual as a bundle of impulses pressing for the satisfaction of immediate as well as historically unmet needs. Since life inevitably denies him this, he develops defenses against those impulses. These defenses become resistances in the treatment, and as they are resolved through verbalization, as the defenses relax and become flexible, the patient becomes aware of his desires and becomes more able to get his needs met. Spotnitz formulated two basic stages in psychic formation, the narcissistic level and the object level. It is at the deepest narcissistic level that the fundamental repetitions are hard-wired and constitute the roots of character. At this level, the origins of psychic structure, the defenses relate to psychic survival; they are erected to deny early object hunger and deprivation. Evidence of this defensive structuring within the patient's mind includes fixations at the levels of fragmentation, externalization, or insistence on oneness. Fragmentation represents a severe degree of damage where the mind is seriously fractured as a result of aggression turned against the self. The fragmented individual lives in a cocoon of chaotic withdrawal. In another defensive posture (externalization), the individual may "eject" the unwanted part of the self into the environment in order to rid the self of unwanted feeling states. Or defending in yet another way, the patient may insist that the object be "just like me." That is, he insists on union with the analyst in order to defend against the feelings of disintegration that may ensue from overstimulation. The primary emotional issues for patients at this narcissistic level involve power, control, and mastery. They want to dominate the object in order to avoid intolerable feeling states. Powerful resistances to influence, even ameliorative influence, are activated. Fears of incorporation or suffocation often lie beneath outbursts of rage and anxiety. The helpless infant struggles mightily to survive. The helpless adult on the couch likewise struggles to get what he needs from the omnipotent figure behind him.

The patient's basic patterns and emotional repetitions, e.g., does he withdraw or attack, does he talk but say nothing or dissolve into despair, are created out of the inevitable frustrations of early maternal interactions, during the first two years of life, before experience can be put into spoken words. During this period emotional pathways are laid down in the deeper layers of the brain, in the area where our animal ancestors live. Spotnitz (1985) notes:

> [T]here is overwhelming evidence of the crucial importance of their [mother and infant] collaborative functioning for personality patterning.... [B]asic homeostatic mechanisms and reciprocal interactions are established within the first months of life through a harmonious relationship between infant and mother; foundations for the ability to love and the ability to learn are rooted in the first 18 months. (pp. 82–83)

> The concomitants of the psychic patterns that operate as obstacles to personality maturation are patterns laid down by early learning in the organ of the mind. (p. 88)

A neuroscientific perspective

Recent neuroscientific research provides the biological underpinnings for this emphasis on the hard-wiring that takes place during the first two years of life. For example, Panksepp (1998), a neuroscientist who has spent his career exploring the basic emotional systems that humans share with other mammals, notes that these systems have to do with fear, rage, panic, and what he calls the "seeking," or motivational, system. These evolutionary systems, according to Panksepp, underlie the higher cognitive apparatus. In fact, Panksepp posits that "a reasonably clear distinction between affective and cognitive processes may exist in the brain, at least in the lower reaches" (p. 39). In other words, Panksepp finds evidence for a primary brain function containing basic emotional systems that predates and forms the infrastructure for the later more refined and sophisticated emotions. Fear, rage, panic, and lust come first. The cognitive superstructure, a later adaptive development, helps create the more tempered and complex emotions, e.g., sadness, guilt, regret, disappointment, and love. According to Panksepp, "Each major emotion has intrinsic response patterning mechanisms, and one of the main functions of higher brain evolution has been to provide ever-greater flexible control over such mechanisms," allowing for greater adaptation (p. 37). Cognition has evolved to advance flexibility and adaptive progress by exerting control over the "lower" systems.

Gerald Edelman (1992), another neuroscientist interested in the origin and processes of consciousness, makes a similar distinction in defining two kinds of consciousness, primary and secondary. Primary consciousness, the brainstem/limbic system that we share with other mammals, evolved primarily to monitor internal bodily functions and is concerned with "appetite, sexual and consummatory behavior, and *evolved defensive behavior patterns*"(p. 117; italics added). The emotional evaluation, memory, and learning that occur in primary consciousness relate to the present, i.e., to immediate pleasure and pain and to reflexive behaviors. Secondary consciousness, the thalamocortical system that connects sensory and other brain signals to the cortex, is very fast in its responses compared to the relatively slow operation of the primary system. According to Edelman, secondary consciousness evolved "to permit increasingly sophisticated motor behavior and the categorization of world events" and through its connection with primary consciousness to generate greater adaptive behavior (p. 118).

Symbolization enables us to have memory of past and future and frees us from the "tyranny of the present" imposed by primary consciousness. To have a subject and a predicate we need a concept of "self" that can be conjured up over time. A whole world of past, present, and future is created once we have both emotional and language centers. As Edelman (1992) explains:

> Higher-order consciousness depends on building a self through *affective intersubjective exchanges*. These interactions...are of the same kind as those guiding semiotic exchange and language building....The result is a model of a world rather than of an econiche, along with models of the past, present, and future. At the same time that higher-order consciousness frees us from the tyranny of

the remembered present, however, *primary consciousness coexists and interacts with the mechanisms of higher-order consciousness. Indeed, primary consciousness provides a strong driving force for higher-order processes. We live on several levels at once.* (p. 150; italics added)

If we were to speculate about how these biological data relate to the concept of psychic change, it makes sense that the pathways forged in the emotive brain structures, the brainstem/limbic system, are not reachable, understandable, or affectable by intellectual means, but rather by emotional messages. Spotnitz (1985) describes this process:

> With the reawakening in the analytic relationship of feelings associated with a significant life experience, "transference behavior" indicates that the specific interneuronal organization set up in response to that experience has been activated. This affords the opportunity to deactivate the pathway originally laid down and to open up other pathways—that is, to connect the emotional state recreated with an interneuronal organization that will express itself in more mature patterns of behavior. (p. 99)

Additionally Spotnitz explains,

> The ultimate goal of the treatment…is to *resolve the behavioral tendencies* that have prevented the patient from reducing these [early growth] needs. With the dissolution of the troublesome patterns, the mental energy that was concentrated on a lower level of functioning becomes available for more mature functioning and future emotional growth. (p. 88)

Observation of the patient's contact function (behavior groping for language) in the transference affords the analyst the opportunity to make these significant interventions.

Countertransference resistance: why umm?

Freud (1910) initially advocated that the analyst remain a *tabula rasa*, a blank receptacle for the patient's fantasies. Any feelings of his own were to be "overcome"(p. 145). His idea was that the analyst was there to help the patient explore all of his thoughts and feelings without the interference of the analyst's personality, which Freud thought would damage the transference and inhibit the communication of unconscious material. His thinking, in essence, was that one could and should get rid of countertransference. In the development of psychoanalytic theory since the 1970s, this idea has changed, and most analysts now regard countertransference as both a source of information as well as a source of potential resistance on the part of the analyst. Given the vicissitudes of unconscious communication, it is difficult to identify a countertransference experience that has nothing at all to do with the patient, but occasionally analysts appear to have instantaneous reactions to certain patients that come solely from their own past and have nothing to do with the patient. That in effect would be called a transference to the patient and needs to be dealt with immediately if the analyst is to work effectively with that patient. Otherwise, countertransference, simply put, is the feelings aroused in the analyst in reaction to the transference of the patient. These feelings are often difficult to experience, and the analyst defends against them, i.e., he develops a countertransference resistance. Umming, or any variety of intervention emanating from the analyst's need to avoid the countertransference feelings and their use for the treatment, constitutes this kind of resistance.

The contact function represents an advance in technique made by Spotnitz and the modern analysts in terms of understanding and managing or controlling countertransference feelings. Countertransference occurs at any time during an analysis and in response to any number of behaviors or expressions of the patient. But countertransference in response to the contact function of the patient takes the analyst to the deepest layers of psychic functioning where the original affective interchanges took place and thus where the primitive defenses developed. The feelings aroused at these levels are extremely difficult for the analyst to tolerate. They include helplessness, hopelessness, and an abysmal aloneness as the patient gropes in his characteristic way for a non-available object. As the analyst is able to tolerate these states and reflect this functioning, he is able to resolve these negative narcissistic resistances first and keep them from being masked by a positive transference. It is this work that frees energy trapped in these defenses for further maturational growth. However, no one wants to feel this helpless, this alone in the world, this out of contact, or to experience any of the states aroused by these defenses. Hence powerful countertransference resistances develop; the analyst umms or executes any variety of intervention designed to avoid or disguise these powerful states. This response can derail an analysis for an extended period of time.

Clinical examples

Individuals trained as modern psychoanalysts are taught from the beginning to wait for, study, and respect the contact function. But as most supervisors know, this is very difficult to do. The student is worried about keeping the patient. He wants to say things that will help her stay in treatment. He often wants to please her, to be liked or admired by her, to help her. He doesn't want to sink into the primitive emotional states of early psychic formation or be hated, ridiculed, attacked, humiliated, ignored, and disregarded. All of these desires coalesce into various countertransference resistances. One of the greatest resistances to the countertransference that beginning students have is the desire to "help" the patient. They are in the field for this very reason. It is therefore extremely difficult to "go backward" with the patient and let her lead the way into a repetitive, often negative and painful state that needs to be worked through before real progress can be made.

Given that following the contact of the patient is the route to knowing and resolving the patient's basic repetitions which lie at the narcissistic levels of functioning, the "Umm" then is a symbolic representation of any kind of intervention that the analyst makes that comes from him as a separate person, from whatever motive makes him ignore the direct contact requirement of the patient. He is thus intervening, not to resolve resistance in the case, but to satisfy some internal motive of his own. This countertransference resistance serves to prevent the analysis from reaching a deeper level. If the student doesn't follow the contact, he may "help" the patient, but he does not really free the psychic structure for growth. That can only occur if the fundamental repetition is resolved. In other words, progress can be made, but at the expense of deeper psychic change. A number of examples illustrate this problem.

A student was studying a silent patient. The patient would come in, lie on the couch, and claim to have nothing to say. The tension would mount. The student insisted that the patient needed him to speak first, to teach him to talk in order to keep the silence from becoming "unbearable." The student tried to wait, but the tension was intolerable. He was afraid that the patient would disintegrate so he would ask questions. The patient made progress. Little by little the patient became more of a "self starter." There was much more talk and reports of life events. The patient finished school, found a job, tried a relationship. However, a careful reading of the student's process recordings revealed that the student was constantly leading this patient, reading his mind, and contacting him at will. The student was unable to wait for the patient's contact and, in fact, felt strongly that the patient was doing well. The patient did seem less depressed and more functional. When the patient decided to leave his maternal home, the student was supportive. He couldn't understand the massive regression that occurred when the patient made the move. Similarly, when the patient tried a relationship, he retreated into a serious withdrawal in response to a relatively minor slight. Clearly, fundamental conflicts were being overlooked. As the student began to discuss his reluctance to wait for the contact, it gradually became clear that he was unable to tolerate the depth of the depressive feelings and the struggle against them that would ensue if he followed the patient's silence. His conflict was intimately connected to events in his own history. As he became aware of this and worked on it in his analysis, and because of his deep desire to help the patient, this student became more and more able to tolerate these states. Now, when the patient occasionally lashed out at him, he was able to reflect this kind of contact, and the patient was able to find an object he could cathect to rather than withdraw from. Frequent hostile interchanges alternated with despair. The student learned to ask a few object-oriented questions rather than try to change the patient's feelings. Little by little the patient's defense loosened, and he became more comfortable verbalizing his negative thoughts and feelings. The effect on his life has been dramatic.

Sometimes the patient's difficulties are so great that the student in training has no chance to wait for the contact. The feelings induced by a very regressed patient can transform the student into a projected part of the patient. A student had been treating an extremely recalcitrant, gruff, burly man who refused to use the couch from the beginning. He also refused to talk, come on time, pay on time, and just about everything else. The student became fascinated with the enormity of the resistance and wanted to write it up as a case study. She decided to take copious notes on the patient's every description of why he wouldn't do anything appropriate including using the couch. Her research revealed fascinating material about the patient's fears: his fear of being submerged, of blowing up, of sexual exploitation, etc. She studied the literature concerning these kinds of fears and resistances and thought that the material she had was significant and revealing about the resistance. Her supervisor tried to help her deal with the patient's resistances, but to no avail. What was wrong here and what does this have to do with the contact function? When the process notes were studied, it was discovered that the patient was in fact conducting the analysis. He was taunting, ridiculing, mocking, directing, and humiliating the analyst. He wouldn't talk until the analyst did what he wanted, i.e., talk first, agree with him, answer his questions, accept his lateness or earliness, etc. He came when he pleased and paid when he pleased. When the student became aware of this, she had great difficulty reversing the pattern. First she was told not to talk until the patient began to talk, to wait for the contact. Often this resulted in 30-minute silences followed by mocking remarks. Later she was told to advise the patient that he had to use the couch or he would have to leave treatment. The student at first found this impossible, but it helped her become aware of her intense fear of this patient. She was afraid of being killed; she was afraid he would leave; she was paranoid about the supervision. Eventually the supervisor told the student she would have to dismiss her as a supervisee. This galvanized the student, and she became able to insist that the patient use the couch. After this, the content of the sessions was completely different from previous sessions with this patient. The ridiculing and mockery were gone. The patient began to talk about real life issues, fantasies, and worries. It remains to be seen what will emerge in response to the contact of this patient, but the work has begun in earnest. Obviously a major countertransference resistance was being acted out, something that can easily occur in working with regressed patients. In this case, the analyst's being unable to work with the contact virtually nullified the analytic work, even though for a long time the student thought differently. The most fascinating aspect of this case to date has been the student's inability to recognize the defiance that this patient was acting out. It was right there in front of her, yet she was completely unconscious of the way it was contorting the treatment. Her focus was entirely on the "interesting content" the patient was producing. As the student becomes able to be in charge and study the contact in the current situation, the basic patterns leading to this massive resistance will be uncovered and worked on.

Another case from my own practice further illustrates this issue. I had been seeing a patient with severe paranoid-schizoid defenses for a number of years. She had moved from a long period of extreme rage reactions to any internal or external disturbance to a state of relatively status quo work on life and relationship problems. However, it had seemed as though the resistance to further progress, to a more cooperative position, was at a standstill. I began to study the sessions more carefully. I noticed that, after ten or fifteen minutes with the woman, I would "Umm." It was so subtle and so habitual as to be almost unconscious. Once I became aware of this, I stopped and remained silent. Suddenly, a huge outburst erupted. "You're not saying anything. What's wrong with you? You're not even there! I can't stand this. Why do I even come? This is horrible! I felt so close to you in here, and now nothing!" During all this, this patient never stopped to contact me or ask me anything. She simply railed on and on at me. I asked her if she could ask me when she'd like me to speak. Further screaming outbursts ensued about the absurdity of this. I realized that this was exactly what the umm was being used to avoid. After the initial years of tolerating this rageful bullying, I'd thought I'd conquered it and worked it through, but obviously I hadn't. I'd been umming to avoid her rage. She remained a person who basically "had a fit" when she didn't get what she wanted. Further, and more importantly, she was still in a deeply narcissistic state. If I didn't say anything, I wasn't there. She needed significantly more work on this problem. I'd lulled myself into thinking that I'd done enough, that she was on her way. Umming kept us stuck, avoiding the rest of the real work to be done. As I was able to change my approach, I was surprised to hear the patient speak tentatively about a drug problem she hadn't wanted to tell me about. The void we'd been avoiding was now uncovered, and it began to fill with the genuine depressive affects she'd run from her whole life. The simple return to following the contact changed this woman's life.

references   Edelman, G. (1992), *Bright Air, Brilliant Fire: On the Matter of Mind.* New York: Basic Books.

Freud, S. (1910), The future prospects of psycho-analytic therapy. *Standard Edition.* London: Hogarth Press, 11:139–152.

Panksepp, J. (1998), *Affective Neuroscience.* Oxford: Oxford University Press.

Spotnitz, H. (1985), *Modern Psychoanalysis of the Schizophrenic Patient.* New York: Human Sciences Press.

Spotnitz, H., L. Nagelberg, & Y. Feldman (1956), Ego reinforcement in the schizophrenic child. *American Journal of Orthopsychiatry,* 26:146–162.

36 Hawthorn Street
Cambridge, MA 02138
maryshepherd@comcast.net

Modern Psychoanalysis
volume **34** number **two 2009**

The epigenesis of psychopathology in children of divorce

Lisa Piemont

In this examination of the impact of divorce on child development, the parents' marriage as a container of the child's emerging affects and drive expressions is identified as crucial to healthy psychological growth of the child. Parental separation and divorce threaten to destabilize child development by removing the needed container and thereby overwhelming the child's immature ego structures with excessive drive energies from within and without. The four cases that are presented examine the psychopathology that may emerge in response to marital dissolution and the interventions that help restore psychic structure. Prevention, the author maintains, requires treatment of the marriage and the child at the earliest sign of marital difficulty.

When the screenwriter Noah Baumbach (2005) dramatized his experience as a child of divorce in the film "The Squid and the Whale," he depicted the parents, Bernard and Joan, as relentlessly pursuing the satisfaction of their own narcissistic needs while remaining blind to the impact of their difficulties on their children. The film narrative follows adolescent Walt and pre-teen Frank through the end of their parents' marriage and into their new life. They must learn to live in two separate households while their mother and father despise one another and fight openly over their children as if they were furniture. Walt and Frank survive, but their efforts to adjust are fueled by sorrow, rage, and fear. Each boy develops defenses to cope with the eruption of intense emotions and drive energies in their parents and in themselves. Walt holds himself together

by forging a powerful identification with his father and an alliance with him against the mother, while Frank, the younger
boy, drifts between the warring factions. He turns to sexual
soothing and discharge of his anger, masturbating and smear-
ing his semen on library books and school lockers, acts that are
desperate efforts to manage his libidinal strivings that have lost
their objects.

Baumbach's story is not unique. Maladaptive responses to
divorce are common, if not the rule. Divorce may ease the
suffering of adults in unsatisfying or painful marriages, but
there is abundant evidence that divorce is harmful to children
when the difficulties between the parents are not resolved.
The impact of a hostile divorce can reverberate throughout
the life of the child (Wallerstein, Lewis, & Blakeslee, 2000).
The danger is that the child's developing ego will be overstimulated, leading to defensive maneuvers to contain the
drives. Overstimulation can come from within; the immature
ego is too fragile to manage id energies without the stabi-
lizing influence of parents who contain their drives through
cathexis to one another. Overstimulation can also come from
without; since the parents' drive energies are intensified by
the narcissistic injury of divorce and no longer cathected to
one another, the child becomes a vulnerable target for their
excesses of drive discharge. Overstimulation in the context of
insufficient insulation of an immature ego is recognized as a
significant source of psychopathology in children and adults
(Spotnitz, 1987).

When children develop symptoms of maladjustment following
divorce, their parents may bring them to therapy to address the
difficulties. Invariably, the parents need therapy themselves to
repair the wounds of marital failure and to learn to create a
healthy environment for their child. This paper presents an
understanding of the role of the marital union and its dissolution in child development and then explores several cases of
"divorced child" therapy in a private practice setting. It examines how an antipathetic divorce can generate specific forms of
damage to a child's developing ego and suggests that child and
family therapy at the earliest onset of marital difficulties may
prevent the more serious forms of maladaptive responses in the
child.

In any relationship in which libidinal and aggressive strivings give rise to love and the wish to connect, hate and the wish to destroy will also arise. Marriage is a dynamic container for the instinctual energies of family life. In marriage, potentially destructive drives may be cathected, contained, and neutralized. The work of marital life must include efforts of the partners to manage their destructive impulses and their hatred for one another and their children in constructive ways. There must be willingness in both partners to resolve conflict and to curtail the acting-out of their aggressive impulses. For instance, partners in a healthy marriage consciously choose to refrain from engaging in hostile conflicts in front of the children. Neither do they displace their frustrations with one another onto their children nor seek libidinal satisfactions from the children rather than from the marriage. If this is accomplished, parents can continue to provide an environment that resembles Bion's (1970) concept of the container and the contained. The marriage is supportive of the child's development toward adulthood as a result of the parents' containment of the child's emerging drives and affects. It is a holding environment in which adult difficulties do not intrude on a child's psychic well-being. The marital container protects the child by maintaining an emotional refuge from the outside world along with at least some protection from the internal storms of normal development as healthy defenses and personality structures emerge.

Winnicott (1965) describes the conditions for healthy development as depending in part on the parents' capacity to identify with their children and to manage their own aggression. These narcissistic identifications make it possible for mothers and fathers to respond to their children's needs by providing the necessary forms of devotion, stability, and cooperation needed for their emotional growth. He also describes the role of the marital union in managing potentially destructive drives that could traumatize the child. The role of the father, he states, is to "draw away from her the element that becomes...potent and spoils the mother's motherliness" (p. 73). Fathers do this by offering support for the mother's positive efforts and validation of the often relentless demands on her capacity for care. They provide mothers with the libidinal supplies that are needed to sustain continuing care of the child. As a result, mothers experience their emotional nutrients as sourced in their partner and feel less depleted. They will still turn to their husbands for support and relief, rather than discharging their frustrations into the relationship with their child or employing a splitting defense in which the child receives all of their libidinal care and the partner, experienced as unavailable, becomes marginalized and cut off from care and concern.

For her part, the emotionally mature mother makes efforts to "draw away" from the father the elements of destructiveness that he may direct toward the child. She intervenes when her partner has reached a point of saturation in responding to a challenging moment with a child. In doing so, she protects both the child and the distraught father from the overstimulation that leads to impulsivity and harm.

Parents in a healthy home sometimes discharge their aggression in the form of jokes shared with one another about the children or by sharing their frustrations with other parents who struggle with the difficult but humorous aspects of child rearing. In either case, children are thereby protected from the discharge of parental drive energies because these are absorbed into the marital union and into other adult relationships.

Failure of the marital union to absorb the psychotic or too potent elements of libidinal and aggressive energies in either parent leaves children susceptible to damage to their developing egos. Anna Freud (1973) remarks that the role of the father is to represent the demands of society as well as to model impulse control. She sees the father as "the embodiment of every sexual and aggressive power, his influence at the same time acts strongly in the direction of repression and transformation of [the child's] instinctual wishes" (p. 639). She describes the father's role as crucial to the development of mature ego functions. When paternal functions are not in place to serve the child's developing ego and superego needs, the child is vulnerable to being flooded by his own drive energies. A father's presence assists both by modeling containment and by containing what is uncontained in the child.

In her studies of children whose fathers were entirely absent from the marital partnership, Freud (1973) describes two responses in the child. On the one hand are children who tend to develop forms of neurotic passivity, wherein they suppress instinctual aims to the point of extinction. On the other hand are children who develop impulse disorders in which instinctual energies are discharged chaotically without sufficient restriction.

In "Treatment of a Pre-schizophrenic Adolescent," Spotnitz (1988) presents the case of Harry Baker, a 13-year-old whose father died when he was five. Even though Harry's mother was unaware that she played a significant role in overstimulating him, thereby preventing his healthy development, she was insightful in identifying from the outset that Harry was in desperate need of a male figure with whom to identify. She requested a Big Brother to help him separate from her, saying, "The thought of hurting me might leave his mind then, and he might stop clinging to me so much" (p. 10). Harry's troublesome development had been provoked by the sudden loss of the parent who had drawn away from him the mother's toxic contents and provided an example of drive-containment.

Even when parents work diligently to discuss the divorce sensitively and supportively with their children, the children invariably react to the news with horror and grief. When a marriage dissolves, children may develop the idea that anger is dangerous and can cause a relationship to end. Consequently, the child's own anger becomes a threat—it is held within, turned against the self, or displaced onto substitute objects. The way in which parents manage their drives and affects, the defenses they employ in order to survive the insult of divorce, is the greatest determinant of the child's response to the trauma. Children of divorce need to know their feelings are heard. They need both parents to accept their anger without the burden of hearing, and thereby absorbing, the parents' hostilities toward one another. Ideally, parents must be available and self-contained, but this is difficult when they themselves are wounded and frightened by the enormity of psychic and material loss consequent to divorce.

When parents are in contention over custody and visitation agreements, they may tend to deny that children need both mother and father fully present and cooperative. Some divorcing parents use questions of custody and visitation to attack one another, making the children's needs secondary to defeating the other parent. These competitive battles that evolve in the winner-takes-all legal strategies for custody and visitation exacerbate children's fears about abandonment, leaving them feeling wounded and emotionally isolated. Only when parents achieve compromise and unity can children grow up free of the traumas imposed by their parents' angry disagreements.

The following clinical cases provide four examples of maladaptive response to the traumatic disruption of divorce. In these cases, obsessional defenses, attacks against the self, impulse disorders, and attention and attachment difficulties emerged when parental hostilities resulted in marital dissolution. Identifying characteristics have been changed to protect the privacy of the children and their families.

A case of obsessional neurosis in an eight-year-old boy

Sam arrived for therapy with his father, Mr. C. In a phone call prior to the session, Mr. C had described Sam's disturbing symptoms. He and Sam's mother had divorced when Sam was four, and Sam's mother had recently remarried and was now on her honeymoon. After she left with her new husband, Sam was seized by the compulsion to wash his hands repeatedly throughout the day. He could not stand physical contact, and if he was touched, he immediately had to wash his hands or hair. He was fearful of others on the street, particularly dark-skinned people. He worried that his father or mother would die and that his new stepfather would murder him and his mother. Sam developed elaborate rituals to fend off his waking nightmares: he repeated phrases from songs, counted a series of numbers over and over, and required himself to repeat specific phrases, such as "Okay, let's go," before he left a room. At the onset of therapy he was unable to go to school because his symptoms had become so disabling.

Sam's mother's marriage to another man evoked a surge of sexual ideas and murderous rage. In one session, he created his own board game, modeled after Monopoly, in which he renamed all the properties, using titles with sexual themes that appeared to remain out of his awareness even as he wrote them down and read them aloud. Worrying that someone would break into his house and attack his mother, he was afraid to go to sleep. His mother's remarriage not only represented a clear break in the relationship with his father, it also gave him a powerful awareness of the mother's sexual impulses. Awareness that his father no longer seemed to have the capacity to attract the mother's drive energies heightened Sam's drives beyond his capacity to contain them. Whenever Sam felt angry with either of his parents, his symptoms returned. His endeavor to gain mastery over this hurricane of instinctual energies led him to create a constellation of rituals and magical ideas that convinced him that he could fend off the threats projected by his fears and impulses.

Sam's experience provides a vivid example of the impact that parental separation can have on psychic structure. Even though his parents had maintained a cooperative relationship after they separated when he was four years old, his mother's remarriage when he was eight caused Sam's young ego to be overwhelmed with anxieties. His reactions were exacerbated when his father remarried a year later. Sam's parents were caught unaware that his mental health relied on their remaining together in his mind. His instinctual energies overwhelmed his ego, and the result was the formation of disabling obsessive and compulsive defenses.

In Sam's therapy he was helped to recognize the relationship between his rage at his parents and the emergence of his symptoms. Sam was helped to join in a project of evidence gathering about his experiences, reporting about events and feelings that preceded symptom episodes. He also agreed to experiment with remedies. When he was experiencing symptoms, he tried to think of things to be angry about even if they weren't immediately identified as problems with his parents. Sam was able to achieve symptom relief by bringing anger to the forefront of his consciousness. Throughout this process of investigation and experimentation, Sam continued to maintain areas in which his parents were protected from being directly targeted with his rage. Due to the fragility of his feelings of attachment to them, Sam continued to worry, consciously and unconsciously, that his rage might cause further abandonment. The therapy has continued over several years, providing Sam with a necessary outlet for his anxieties and drive energies. His parents cooperated by following the suggestion that they welcome and validate Sam's angry and blaming feelings about his experience as a child of divorce. Sam no longer needs the symptom formation to cope with his drive energies although he continues to use the therapy as a source of support and a container in which he can discharge his frustration aggression.

A series of attacks against the self in a six-year-old girl

Emma was brought for therapy following the death of her older sister. The therapy initially involved talking about loss and death. Emma used art materials to draw pictures for the lost sister and to make storybooks about her sister's illness. Emma was concerned about her parents' well-being. In their preoccupation with their own pain and grief, they were having a difficult time meeting Emma's needs and the needs of her two brothers. The children acted out to get attention, only to receive anger and impatience in return. Emma's mother also reported that she and Emma's father were verbally and physically violent with one another.

Emma appeared to benefit from the attention she got in the therapy sessions and from working on her own grief. In sessions, Emma made "cookies" out of paper or clay and baked them in an oven fashioned out of construction paper. The oven was saved and reused each week as she baked elaborate confections for her mother. It seemed she was trying to feed her mother's emotional hunger as well as to enact a fantasy of the feedings she wanted for herself. Sadly, three years after the death of her sister, Emma's parents announced that they were divorcing. Her father, a pastor, blamed her mother, excoriating her in front of the children for going against his beliefs. In reaction Emma developed a new symptom, compulsive overeating. This set off a battle with her mother over her consumption of food.

In her sessions, Emma began to bake cookies solely for herself. Her food preparations expanded to making meals of every kind, but these gifts were no longer offered to her mother at the close of the sessions as they had been prior to the parents' separation. Her mother reported that Emma was hoarding food under her bed and in other secret locations. Her hunger for love and oral gratification exploded beyond bounds. Next, Emma began to pull her hair out. Starting with her eyebrows and expanding to her hairline, she compulsively removed her hair by the roots. She said she could not stop, that it both hurt and felt good to wound herself in this way. This led to her becoming the victim of severe teasing at school and to the loss of her ability to retain friends as a source of comfort and reassurance during this difficult time. She adopted periodic muteness, thereby symbolically mirroring the withholding she felt was directed at her by her parents' refusal to maintain the marriage. This behavior further frustrated her mother into rages.

In Emma's case, her parents' divorce as preceded by her sister's death made for a tenuous internal structure that became exhausted by her fears of loss and abandonment. Emma turned her aggressive and libidinal drives against herself. She cathected the comforts provided by biting and chewing great quantities of food, and she turned her aggressive drive onto her body. Emma's hair pulling seemed to be an intense effort to symbolically and literally tear herself apart. Emma substituted her own immature ego for the container that her parents' marriage had been. Sadly, her defensive structures were not prepared to manage the intensity of the drives and affects that emerged when she became terrified of abandonment. She resorted to relentless attacks on her body, a perverse solution to the need for libidinal comforts and aggressive discharge.

In Emma's treatment, the therapist reflected and mirrored the motivations for Emma's behaviors. Emma was helped to understand that her hunger was emotional and valid in the circumstances in which she had come to feel invisible and powerless. The therapist functioned as her narcissistic twin, also hungry, fearful, and in need of love. This mirroring enabled Emma to share the overwhelming burden her immature ego had taken on, allowing her to develop fantasy and play as outlets for her drive energies. The following excerpt illustrates a typical interaction designed to assist Emma in alleviating the pressure her drives were exerting on her fragile ego.

P: [Emma is making cookies out of construction paper and clay, describing what she wants them to be like—both pretty and appetizing.] This one is going to have a heart on it. This one will be a face—a smiley face. This one will be just sprinkles. Lots and lots and lots of sprinkles! [She attends to the decorations.]

A: Yum!

P: Oh, yes. You can have some, but you have to wait.

A: Oh, but I'm so hungry. [Emma smiles.] I'm really, really hungry. I don't think I can wait.

P: Well, you have to wait. I'm putting them in the oven now.

A: They look good. Are they almost ready?

P: Yes, they are. They're ready to come out.

A: Oh, they look so good. I am really, really hungry [smiles] Can I have one now?

P: Sure. You can have... [Now she has a hard time choosing one for the therapist.]

A: Is there enough for me?

P: [nods] I'm going to have this one and this one and this one. This one's for my mom. So, you can have this one.

A: Do we eat them now?

P: Yes! [There is dramatic aggressive eating until all the cookies are shredded. A deflated mood emerges.]

A: They're gone. [Emma nods.] What if I'm still hungry?

P: [smiling and invigorated] We can make some more. I *have* to make some for my mom.

A: Moms need cookies and lots of them!

P: [Begins a new round of cookie creating.] My mom likes hearts, so this one's for her. Are you gonna make some, too?

A: Should I?

P: Yeah! You're hungry, aren't you?

A: Yeah. But sometimes I feel hungry even when I'm full.

P: I know. [Becoming quiet, she slows down her cookie making.] I wanna go see my mom. [Gets up to go to the waiting room where her mother sits. She makes physical contact.
There are hugs, and she returns to the office.] Can we play a
game? I wanna play War.

Emma was reassured by this contact with her mother in the
waiting room. Seeing that her fantasies surrounding eating and
baking had not harmed her mother, she felt free to express her
aggression. A competitive round of the card game War ensued,
and Emma was able to talk about some anger she felt with her
mother for leaving her father. The use of joining, mirroring,
and psychological reflection provided Emma with an experience of containment that had been absent since her parents
separated (Spotnitz, 1987).

An impulse disorder persisting into adulthood

Steven, now 36, grew up as the oldest son of three. His biological father, for whom he was named, left when he was nine,
and his mother soon remarried. Steven described his mother
as chronically unhappy and unable to give him any tender-
ness. Blaming him for his father's departure, she told him
repeatedly that she wished he had never been born. She produced two daughters with her second husband, who was rarely
present and finally left when Steven was 12. Mother required
Steven to babysit for his half-sisters during the afternoons.
Without personal activities or interests, his concept of himself
as unlovable solidified. He made few friends at school, and
entering adolescence, he made no effort to seek out relationships with girls the way his peers were doing. Instead, in acts
of rage against his mother and in a vain attempt to have the
sexual experiences he thought his peers were enjoying, Steven
sexually molested both his sisters.

Having no father with whom to identify, no father who could
offer him protection from his mother's rages by drawing them
onto himself, Steven was burdened with sexual and aggressive
impulses that stormed inside him, and he lacked outlets or defensive structures for their containment. Attacks on his sisters,
the only persons in his environment more powerless than he,

provided outlets for the discharge of sexual and aggressive energies that were beyond his control.

Convicted of sexual assault, Steven spent six years in prison. In group therapy sessions he attended there, the only emotional state he could identify for several years was anger. But with the help of group members, he learned about the other emotions that fueled his abundant tension. He began to talk about neglect and rejection by his mother and about how imprisoned he felt himself to be by his mother's unhappiness. In outpatient treatment, he sought approval and encouragement hungrily, as if starved for these nutrients. However, he expressed disinterest in his own life progress and satisfaction, having possibly adopted and internalized his mother's death wish toward him.

Steven harbored a deep reservoir of anger. Whenever his power and autonomy were threatened, he lashed out verbally and physically without hesitation. At his jobs he responded to slights with inordinate rage. In social situations, terrified of the intensity of the libidinal energies that were pressing for expression, Steven suffered from extreme shyness. Steven's dynamics demonstrate a common outcome of parental separation: distorted ego and superego development force the discharge of primitive drive energies into impulsive attacks on others and on one's self.

Steven's progress in treatment seemed to arise from his motivation to reach for an ego-ideal that represented specific positive values that he gleaned from his experience in group work with other men: honesty, integrity, loyalty, intelligence, and respect. His drive energies became cathected with these ideals so that when he spoke about them he became passionate. The values came to embody a kind of composite, ideal paternal object; binding his drive energies to this ideal incrementally strengthened his ego. Though a certain rigidity remained in his superego functions, he was able to release tension through humor in the form of self-deprecation. He identified the need for adequate levels of insulation to alleviate the impact of his critical superego functions, and became able to acknowledge his need for time alone to care for his animals, to exercise, and to play fantasy football. With this defense in place, Steven was able to keep his tension levels within a manageable range.

In Steven's case, it was his own talking in the facilitating environment of the therapy hour that enabled him to develop the mature personality structures that had been underdeveloped since childhood (Winnicott, 1965). Mirroring interventions by the therapist were designed to tame his harsh superego, while joining techniques provided insulation for his drive energies (Spotnitz, 1987). In therapy sessions, Steven often said, "I'm a piece of shit." or "I'm an asshole." The therapist replied to these assessments with: "Okay, let me see if I've got this straight: you're a soft, brown, smelly pile of excrement?" or "You're just a shit factory?" Steven responded, "Well, when you put it that way, what I mean is…" and countered the self-attack with a more tempered analysis of his character. Recently, he has been able to point out a mistake he might have made without expressing such intense anger with himself. His ego has strengthened in the transference, and feelings have emerged that were absent in his early life such as the feeling of being worthwhile and wanted.

Attention problems and attachment disorder in a twelve-year-old girl

When Martina reached the age of four soon after immigrating to this country from Romania, her parents got divorced. The divorce was followed by a campaign on her father's part to win her over as a victory trophy in his battle against her mother. He seductively plied Martina with gifts and permissiveness to make himself the preferred parent. When Martina complained about minor conflicts with her mother, he supported and exaggerated them, and then added his own negative thoughts. He objected to any expression of affection Martina might make toward her mother. He cried and clung to her when they parted at the end of her visitations.

Martina's mother responded to Martina's negative moods and complaints about their time together with hostile retaliation, a displacement of her anger toward Martina's father whom she perceived as turning Martina against her with his emotional neediness. In response to feeling insecure in the relationships with both of her parents, Martina developed severe anxiety attacks. At visiting time with her mother, she would crawl under her bed and cry inconsolably until her father returned to pick her up. She chose to spend more time with her father, and her mother eventually gave up trying to make her own time with Martina successful. These difficulties were exacerbated by the isolation Martina experienced as a newcomer to this country, learning a new language while attempting to forge friendships with peers.

Martina was essentially erased as an individual in her own right. Her father used her as his confidante in place of his wife. She was his source of security and love. Simultaneously her mother ceased to see her as anything but an extension of the father's hostile campaign to discredit her as a woman and a parent. Constrained by her parents' ceaseless narcissistic demands, Martina's own need for security and love was squelched.

When she was brought in for treatment at age 19, Martina was having severe difficulties in school with both learning objectives and peer relationships. Although she had acquired fluency in English, she was not motivated to complete her homework. She seemed unable to sustain effort at working for longer than a few minutes at a time. In class, she drifted off, left her seat, and detached from what was occurring in the classroom. She was completely lost in her own emotional world. Martina was diagnosed with Attention Deficit Disorder and given medication. This reduced her impulsivity, but she seemed to turn even further inward, becoming obsessively preoccupied with her body image.

In sessions, Martina alternated between three types of presence: a withdrawn state of examining objects in her purse; a seductive demeanor characterized by her asking intrusive questions about the therapist's sexual experiences; or a hostile demeanor featuring paranoid accusations and angry threats to leave. Whereas the active roles of seducer or attacker seemed to represent imitations of her parents, the withdrawn state seemed to be her most authentic self.

In Martina's case, internalizations of parental representations had occurred, but they were of a part-object, one-dimensional, and primitive nature. Her father's affective seductions and manipulations and her mother's hostile rejection and abandonment became the only models for attachment Martina could

draw upon. This made the development of secure relationships with peers and teachers impossible. When her academic
and disciplinary problems exceeded the capacity of her public
school's resources, Martina was referred by her school for residential care.

The treatment approach in Martina's case involved intensive
work with the parental dyad. Both parents became motivated
by their shared goal of having a healthy child—a goal that met
their narcissistic need to be mirrored in the world. They will-
ingly learned to avoid engaging in destructive patterns, and
instead began presenting their daughter with a positive impres-
sion of their relationship as cooperative and mutually supportive. This helped reduce Martina's anxiety about their aggression
toward each other as well as her own fears about their abandoning her. Her energy was freed to forge an identity of her own,
using the healthier aspects of her parents' personalities that
emerged when the destructive elements were contained. After
Martina's return from the residential program, she enrolled in
a therapeutic day school. Her parents were now better prepared
to cooperate in her care. She has resided with both parents in
a joint custody agreement since then, and the parents continue
to attend conjoint sessions on her behalf.

Conclusion

These case vignettes are representative of the lives of countless
children whose development has been disrupted by marital
disharmony and divorce. Something crucial is lost internally
for a child when his parents' relationship deteriorates and dissolves. His psychic structures are weakened by the excessive
demands that the losses of divorce place on his developing
ego. In addition to difficulties in developing a healthy attachment style and managing uncontained drive energies, the
child is frequently overwhelmed by feelings of powerlessness
and insignificance. This experience is symbolized in Baumbach's movie by the image of Walt's visiting the exhibit of the
giant squid fighting the giant whale at the Museum of Natural
History in New York. Walt is dwarfed by the creatures' size
and the inexorable nature of their battle as they remain fro-
zen for all time in a death grip, just as his parents seemed

to be. For Walt's real-life counterparts, much of the solution appears to lie in the possibility of therapeutic remediation of their relationship.

Donner (2006) found that divorce represents a narcissistic injury and a psychic loss to each parent, leaving each no longer feel loved or wanted. Their libidinal needs then turn toward the child. Any expression of love on the child's part toward the other parent is experienced as a threat and a loss of control. With their aggressive impulses evoked by the perception that they cannot win the child as their sole possession and feeling the threat of loss of narcissistic supplies now sourced in the child, parents concern themselves with what they are "getting" in the divorce. The number of days and hours they have with their child is entered onto a psychic scoreboard, and the child's personal needs, such as a daughter's need for more time with mother during puberty, are forgotten. As a result, children become overstimulated by the open expression of their parents' libidinal and aggressive strivings. They are equally overwhelmed by the abundance of their own drive energy that has been set loose by the parents' decision to destroy the container of the familial bond. Terrified of the aggression in the environment and in themselves, they are left to forge strategies for survival with whatever primitive defenses may be at their disposal.

The therapist's role in treating divorced parents is to model "good-enough" mothering (Winnicott, 1965). The therapist models the healthy parent, absorbing and containing drive energies of the dyad, raising awareness of the child's needs and of the impact of parental actions, both verbal and physical, on the child's well-being. The narcissistic need of each parent to be loved by the child as reflected in the child's allegiance can be transformed into the goal of being positively reflected by the child's emotional stability and proper functioning in the world. The therapist can support this trend by building a shared vision of the child's innate gifts and noticing the obstacles that might lie in the way of the child's ability to express those gifts in the world. For example, parents can be helped to become flexible about visitation arrangements when traveling between homes twice a week impedes academic and extracurricular activities during the high school years.

In order to improve cooperation between parents who have themselves been injured by the experience of one another's rejection and attacks, the therapist must routinely offer narcissistic supplies, working to reverse patterns of harm that may have been chronic through many years of a troubled marriage. McCormack (2000) discusses important moments when the therapist acts as an assistant to the couple, helping them move away from the paranoid-schizoid position of splitting and projective identification. They are encouraged instead to adopt the therapist's capacity to think rather than act and to consider alternatives to the binary, either-or mode of thinking that dominates pre-oedipal personality organization. As the therapy offers a transitional space for contemplation rather than action, couples begin to experience one another as less threatening, and collaboration in the care of the children can more easily occur.

For example, a divorced couple sought treatment for their impulse-disordered 12-year-old son, but in the first session it became evident that their own relationship was severely contaminated by unmitigated rage, contempt, and vengeful retaliation, behaviors that were demonstrated in each of their early sessions. Taking a position of thoughtful curiosity, the therapist presented a theory that their son's difficulties might be directly related to the models they exhibited in their interactions in her office. As a result of examining these patterns, they began to work more humanely with one another to resolve long-standing disputes about custody and to identify their own well-being as co-parents as central to their child's mental health. Progress in the case came in part from the therapist's demonstrations of positive regard for both parents, even in the face of their mutual contempt. A respectful disposition firmly placing limits on acting out in the session neutralized the couple's hostile aggression and made it possible for effective dialogue to begin.

In the treatment of children who are suffering from the impact of divorce and its aftermath, the therapist offers an experience of consistency, drive containment, and affect tolerance as an alternative to what the child may be experiencing in his family life. In play and in conversation, the child's drives and affects are expressed and explored without condemnation. The child's overwhelming experience of loss and powerlessness, which often cannot be held by either parent, can find expression in the therapy when the therapist encourages unique and creative avenues for empowerment and mastery of the child's internal and external worlds.

The basic human need to feel wanted was poignantly expressed and worked through in the case of Harry Baker (Spotnitz, 1988). Harry threatened to abandon the treatment if the analyst would not agree to adopt him. He was suffering from powerlessness that stemmed from a history of insecure attachments. When it was suggested that he could adopt the analyst, Harry felt empowered to choose the relationship for himself, thereby stemming the anxiety about possible abandonment by a needed other. In therapy, the child of divorce also suffers from intense fears of abandonment and is helped when he can express his objections and anger about the loss of the marital union and about the resulting feelings of not being wanted by either parent, feelings that occur no matter how many assurances parents have offered to the contrary.

Children of divorce benefit from treatment from the very onset of their parents' rift. At the same time, parents must be educated about the impact of their hostilities on their children and helped to work together for the children's well-being. An explicit understanding of the effects of divorce on children can help parents manage their affects and drive energies in more mature ways and become motivated to utilize options such as mediation rather than litigation to resolve differences about custody and visitation. They can make every effort to maintain for their children the experience of being fully contained.

references   Bion, W. (1970), *Attention and Interpretation*. New York: Jason Aronson.

Baumbach, N. (2005), *The Squid and the Whale*. Culver City, CA: Sony Pictures.

Donner, M. (2006), Tearing the child apart: the contribution of narcissism, envy, and perverse modes of thought to child custody wars. *Psychoanalytic Psychology,* 23(3):542–553.

Freud, A. & D. T. Burlingham (1973), *Infants without Families: Reports on the Hampstead Nurseries, 1939–1945*. Vol. III of *The Writings of Anna Freud*. New York: International Universities Press.

McCormack, C. C. (2000), *Treating Borderline States in Marriage: Dealing With Oppositionalism, Ruthless Aggression, and Severe Resistance.* . Northvale, NJ: Jason Aronson.

Spotnitz, H. (1987), *Psychotherapy of Preoedipal Conditions: Schizophrenia and Severe Character Disorders.* Northvale, NJ: Jason Aronson.

Spotnitz, H. (1988), Treatment of a pre-schizophrenic adolescent: case presentation on the reconstruction of a psychotic ego. *Modern Psychoanalysis.* 13(1):3–200.

Wallerstein, J. S., J. M. Lewis, & S. Blakeslee (2000), *The Unexpected Legacy of Divorce: A 25 Year Landmark Study.* New York: Hyperion.

Winnicott, D. W. (1965), *The Family and Individual Development.* London: Tavistock

The epigenesis of psychopathology in children of divorce **Lisa Piemont**

95 Summit Avenue, 2nd Floor
Summit, NJ 0790
lpiemont@mbrac.com

Book review

Searching for the Perfect Woman: The Story of a Complete Psychoanalysis. V. D. Volkan with J. C. Fowler. Lanham, MD: Jason Aronson, 2009. 157 pp.

Searching for the Perfect Woman provides a surprisingly complete recounting of a five-year, four-day-a-week psychoanalysis, begun when the male patient was 57 years old. The author, a renowned analyst, not only describes the steady incremental progress of his patient, but also courageously reveals the substance of his interventions and his rationale for choosing them. The narrative is periodically interrupted by very astute questions posed by J. Christopher Fowler, a one-time colleague of Volkan's at the Austen Riggs Center in Stockbridge, Massachusetts. Fowler's questions echo those that may very likely be forming in the reader's mind, providing an opportunity for Volkan to explain his theoretical and technical stance to the reader as the case unfolds. The result is a book of great value to both the experienced analyst and the beginning student of analysis, for the reader gets to see what the analyst is grappling with, how he makes sense of it, and why he chooses to intervene in the manner he does. Volkan's choice of interventions may elicit criticism from those steeped in technical orientations different from his, but if the proof is in the pudding, the case as described certainly has a positive outcome, lending credence to Volkan's rationale. At the very least, the extensive account of Volkan's interventions provides a fecund starting point for discussion of psychoanalytic technique.

Volkan gives the name "Hamilton" to the patient he presents in this book. Hamilton, a successful Southern industrialist obsessed with sleeping with a different woman every single night (hence the title of the book), endured a difficult—even lurid—childhood, despite having been born into a "first family of Virginia" with attendant wealth and stature. By an odd twist of fate and heritage, the patient's grandmother was an ardent believer in the child-rearing techniques propounded by Dr. Schreber, the very same child-rearing techniques endured by the subject of Freud's 1925 study "Psycho-analytic Notes on an Autobiographical Account of a Case of Paranoia." Hamilton's grandmother's active participation in his child-rearing (and her profound influence on her son and daughter-in-law, Hamilton's parents, in that regard) resulted in weekly torture sessions ostensibly designed to build Hamilton's character. After the Sunday afternoon meal, Hamilton's grandmother would lecture his parents on the importance of teaching children the "art of renouncing." Hamilton's mother would go out to the garden to cut "suitable branches" with which to whip Hamilton—which she did until he "renounced" crying. After this, Hamilton and his brother were taken upstairs to the bathroom where their father beat their bare buttocks with a razor strop, crying "This hurts me more than it hurts you!" This harsh treatment contrasted sharply with the loving care lavished upon Hamilton by his beloved Abigail, an African-American nanny who was peremptorily dismissed without explanation when Hamilton was four years old.

Volkan presents these historical details—and many others—without conveying the idea that they are directly responsible for Hamilton's current psychic difficulties. Rather, they are presented—along with many vivid dreams and reports from the patient's everyday affairs—as currency proffered by the patient in the psychoanalytic process, to be taken as products of the patient's psyche and consequently as clues to what interventions would be the most therapeutic. Because the historical elements are recounted chronologically, the story unfolds in the fashion of a detective mystery, narrated and decoded by a disciplined analyst seeking the meaning of the presented clues.

Volkan's (1976) text, *Primitive Internalized Object Relations: A Clinical Study of Schizophrenic, Borderline and Narcissistic Patients*, reveals his object relations orientation along with an intense interest in using psychoanalysis to work with the same body of patients that inspired Spotnitz. In this early work, Volkan's technique remained firmly in the interpretive camp: "Interpretation is the analyst's basic tool in dealing with both neurotic and psychotic patients in psychoanalytic treatment" (p. 95). While Volkan does acknowledge in this early text that "analysis of the

Oedipal conflicts must await resolution of pre-genital conflicts," he says that, "What is initially significant for the psychotic is *systematic interpretation that basically provides differentiation of the analytic introject from his archaic objects*" (p. 96; italics added). While this language suggests the implicit assumption of a narcissistic transference and the need to resolve it, it also essentially casts the analyst in the role of teacher interacting with the patient on an intellectual plane. Volkan writes:

> What lies on the surface of the patient's relatedness to his analyst in full psychotic transference, i.e., cannibalistic fantasies relating to introjection, are manifestations of what we would call "deep material" in the case of a neurotic patient. *The analyst should not, I believe, shy away from interpretations* about such manifestations from the point of view of object relations, since it is helpful for the patient to have his uncanny fantasies and experiences given a name, and designated as events in a developmental process rather than as grotesque occurrences taking place outside human experience. Such interpretation also assists the patient as he learns how to tame his aggressive impulses, and gives him ideas concerning libidinal involvement. (p. 97; italics added)

Volkan would probably acknowledge that the technical approach depicted in the current volume has significantly evolved from the version he espoused in his early text. Moreover, he seems to have a firm grasp of what the modern psychoanalyst would call the narcissistic transference and the importance of allowing it to develop without interference from interpretive input from the analyst. He now writes:

> It is most important that an analyst be patient! As a psychoanalyst, I don't interpret everything I see. I let the psychoanalytic processes develop. Creating an analytic space in which [the patient] is free to experience emotions and fantasies, to cast me in the image of a bad mother and a dangerous father, is critical.... [At the beginning of treatment] we can be content to "invite" [the patient] to develop an experience of the various transferences by remaining curious, attentive and receptive. (pp. 18–19)

In short, Volkan's technique has evolved so as to at least implicitly acknowledge the potentially injurious impact of interpretation on the patient with a narcissistic personality organization.

> All patients sense that psychoanalysis will take away their established way of handling mental conflicts and anxiety and force them to face these conflicts and feel unpleasant emotions connected with them. This is why they resist "hearing" the analyst's

interpretations of what is going on in their internal worlds. Instead...they depend on their own way of subduing unpleasant emotions, even though they continue to ask for help, and pay the analyst's fee. (p. 24)

Nonetheless, Volkan's interpretive roots remain. The following is his account of an extended intervention from early in Hamilton's analysis. While demonstrating an implicit wariness of overstimulating the patient, it reveals a strong interest in forging a "therapeutic alliance" and a concomitant preference for a pedagogical stance.

Some months after he began working with me, I explained [to the patient], without accusing him, how his morning activities and "free associations" during his sessions were serving his resistance to analytic work. Even while I was explaining this to him, I knew that he would understand what I said only on an intellectual level. He "heard" me, but gave no emotional response and continued with his morning ritual and his style of "free associations," as well as with his "chopping up" of himself, his women, me, and his sessions. Then I repeated out loud that his visiting Abigail and Morris every morning appeared to be a response to an internal "*need*," and not to a simple "*wish*." I explained to him that re-finding Abigail each morning was like finding fresh air to breathe. Otherwise, he would feel choked as if he were in a burning building. I asked him to remain curious about what I said to check his mind to see when his motivation for this morning behavior would become a "*wish*" instead of remaining a "*need*." I suggested that when his "*need*" became a "*wish*," he might be ready to have a "choice," and modify and/or even give up his daily meetings with the representations of his childhood love objects. This made him feel relaxed and more comfortable with me. I was not pushing him. I was emphatically understanding him and showing him choices. (p. 25; italics added)

Conveying to the patient early in the analysis that he is "understood" and that the analyst has the intent of "showing him choices" not only signals an implicit assumption that the patient's mental organization is amenable to such a rational approach, but it also suggests that Volkan wants to be seen only as benevolent and that he may be reluctant to elicit a negative transference. Later in the book, Volkan does endorse the notion that the patient's verbalization of aggression in the analytic session is appropriate and necessary:

As an analyst, you have to be confident that...negative imagery [about the analyst] is part of [the patient's] conscious and unconscious work. You don't want to shy away from the negative and only join when the patient senses you as a good object. I see this failure in supervision quite frequently…I tell the therapist to relax and listen to the story that is unfolding. I try to help the therapist understand why they [*sic*] are so averse to the anger of the patient. (p. 61)

But Volkan's recommended response seems to consist solely of calm explanation of the aggression and an attempt to elicit the patient's curiosity about its origins. For example, when Hamilton confided a childhood fantasy of wanting to insert an enema tube into a black woman's anus to blow her up and explode her, the patient, upon hearing an interpretation, immediately became silent, apparently "paralyzed with fear." Volkan reports what ensued:

> After waiting a few minutes for him to relive the impact of his anxiety, I told him that he might wish to give an enema to Michelle [his current girlfriend] and explode her. I added that while he was able to…experiment to sleep with her two nights in a row, she, like his other many previous women, could still, in his mind, turn out to be "bad." I said: "No wonder your childhood image blowing up a woman, Abigail [his beloved nanny] who rejected you has come to your mind." [Hamilton] murmured: "Sweet revenge!" But then he felt paralyzed again. After a while, he began to speak of a businessman of Turkish origin… [who] was modest and polite. (p. 54)

At this juncture, Volkan chooses to interpret *further*:

> I chose to tell Hamilton that this "Turk" represented *me*. [Volkan is originally from Turkey.] I told Hamilton that he was changing me into a *gentle* Turk because he was still afraid of rejections, beatings, homosexual attacks, and torture if he experienced his childhood rage, "like blowing up a woman through putting an enema tube into her anus." I asked him if he could tolerate imagining that he not only wanted to urinate and defecate on *me*, but [that] he wanted to put an enema tube into *me* and also use me as a target for his sperm bullets and "kill" *me* like he wanted to kill Dorothy [his sister], his rejecting mother, his big brother who might approach him sexually in the bed they shared, and his scary father in the "torture chamber." I wondered out loud what kind of guarantee he needed in order to express his negative thoughts and feelings openly without an expectation of punishment. Then I added that he might consider that such thoughts and feelings, which he could not name when he was a child, might be dealt with playfully since he was now an adult. I also told Hamilton that I would tolerate such thoughts and feelings *if he would*." (pp. 54–55; italics added.)

An analyst trained in the technique of Spotnitz might very well find this onslaught of insight and prescription to be troubling, especially when Volkan simultaneously acknowledges that "*for Hamilton it is an awful thing to think of aggressive things.... he still cannot distinguish between feeling and fantasy on the one hand and reality in action on the other. It is a thin distinction for him. He fears actually harming me if he fantasizes about blowing me up. The infantile fantasies of childhood still frighten him... his affective life is too frightening to him—it is too real*" (p. 55). But Volkan apparently believes that interpretations provide fodder for the patient's nascent curiosity and that becoming curious about one's mental life is a key element of psychoanalysis: "*I tell him [the patient] it is like a play. I give him the freedom to play...with me. As long as I don't introduce or create the play or force a story line on him, he can create his own therapeutic stories or plays*" (p. 55). Inherent in this outlook and, indeed, in the entire book, is the author's acknowledgment that transference and repetition are the building blocks of the "plays" created by the patient and that pent-up aggression is encapsulated in them. But Volkan does not explain how psychic change is engendered by the interpretive approach just cited.

Concerning the emotional impact on the analyst of the patient's aggression, Volkan appears to believe that it is sufficient for the analyst to be able to *tolerate* the patient's aggression; he does not venture into the realm of the therapeutic use of the analyst's real feelings or emotional communication from analyst to patient: "*I was confident that I could tolerate his murderous rage for me because I was analyzed and I had been in the professional business of analyzing others for many years. One anxious person in the room is enough. As long as I am not anxious about his fantasies and feelings, I will remain in the role as his analyst*" (p. 55). The reader is prompted to wonder what would happen if Volkan *did* become anxious during session (and stray from what he considers the role of analyst to be) or, more importantly, what defenses are in place that prevent him from feeling anxiety in the session.

Nevertheless, by the end of this fascinating book it seems clear that Hamilton has made great progress, giving up obsessive infantile repetitive behaviors, forging new and mature relationships, and relating to his analyst, his family, and everyone else in his life in an authentic and feelingful manner. However, as always in assessments of case presentations, what cannot be said for certain is whether it was Volkan's interpretive approach that was responsible for Hamilton's transformation or whether it was some other perhaps elusive factor (or combination of factors) that contributed to Hamilton's emotional maturation. Volkan's patience and self-restraint, his receptivity and resolute curiosity, his calm demeanor, and the emotional impact of his interpretations (as opposed to their intellectual content) were all potentially influential. But whatever conclusions are eventually drawn, Volkan has provided students of psychoanalysis with a rich body of material to ponder.

Stephen R. Guttman

references   Volkan, V. D. (1979), *Primitive Internalized Object Relations: A Clinical Study of Schizophrenic, Borderline and Narcissistic Patients.* New York: International Universities Press.

Books received

Akhtar, Salman. *Comprehensive Dictionary of Psychoanalysis*. London: Karnac, 2009. 403 pp.

Akhtar, Salman. *The Damaged Core: Origins, Dynamics, Manifestations, and Treatment*. Lanham, MD: Jason Aronson, 2009. 229 pp.

Bersani, Leo. *Is the Rectum a Grave? and Other Essays*. Chicago: The University of Chicago Press, 2010. 211 pp. softcover.

Cartwright, Duncan. *Containing States of Mind: Exploring Bion's "Container Mode" in Psychoanalytic Psychotherapy*. New York: Routledge, 2010. 274 pp. softcover.

Dean, Tim. *Unlimited Intimacy: Reflections on the Subculture of Barebacking*. Chicago: University of Chicago Press, 2009. 237 pp. softcover.

Gerson, Mary-Joan. *The Embedded Self: An Integrative Psychodynamic and Systemic Perspective on Couples and Family Therapy*. 2nd ed. New York: Routledge, 2009. 291 pp. softcover.

Ferro, Antonia & Roberto Basile, eds. *The Analytic Field: A Clinical Concept*. London: Karnac, 2009. 223 pp. softcover.

Heller, Mary Brownescombe & Sheena Pollet, eds. *The Work of Psychoanalysis in the Public Health Sector*. New York: Routledge, 2010. 219 pp. softcover.

Huprich, Steven, ed. *Narcissistic Patients and New Therapists: Conceptualization, Treatment, and Managing Countertransference*. Lanham, MD: Jason Aronson, 2008. 134 pp.

Jacobsen, Kurt. *Freud's Foes: Psychoanalysis, Science, and Resistance*. Lanham, MD: Rowman & Littlefield, 2009. 187 pp.

Kakar, Sudhir. *Mad and Divine: Spirit and Psyche in the Modern World*. Chicago: University of Chicago Press, 2009. 178 pp.

124 Katchadourian, Herant. *Guilt: The Bite of Conscience.* Stanford, CA: Stanford University Press, 2010. 370 pp.

Kohut, Heinz. *The Analysis of the Self: A Systematic Approach to the Psychoanalytic Treatment of Narcississtic Personality Disorder.* Chicago: The University of Chicago Press, 2009. 368 pp. softcover.

Kohut, Heinz. *The Restoration of the Self.* Chicago: The University of Chicago Press, 2009. 344 pp. softcover.

Rangell, Leo. *Music in the Head: Living at the Brain-Mind Border.* London: Karnac, 2009. 93 pp.

Silverman, Kaja. *Flesh of My Flesh.* Stanford, CA: Stanford University Press, 2009. 272 pp. softcover.

Stepansky, Paul E. *Psychoanalysis at the Margins.* New York: Other Press, 2000. 357 pp.

Stern, Donnel. *Partners in Thought: Working with Unformulated Experience, Dissociation, and Enactment.* New York: Routledge, 2010. 229 pp. softcover.

Volkan, Vamik D. with Christopher Fowler. *Searching for the Perfect Woman: The Story of a Complete Psychoanalysis.* Lanham, MD: Jason Aronson, 2009. 157 pp.

Wagner, Barry M. *Suicidal Behavior in Children and Adolescents.* New Haven: Yale University Press, 2009. 314 pp. softcover.

Contributors

HOLMES, LUCY, Ph.D., is a licensed psychoanalyst in private practice in New York City. A graduate of the Center for Modern Psychoanalytic Studies, she serves there as a faculty member and training analyst. She is past president of the Society of Modern Psychoanalysts. Formerly executive director of the Center for Group Studies, she currently teaches in its weekend training program. She is author of *The Internal Triangle: New Theories of Female Development* as well as numerous articles, many on women and women's groups..

KALIN, EUGENE B., Ph.D., is a licensed psychoanalyst and marriage and family therapist in private practice in New York City and Great Neck, NY. Dr. Kalin is a training analyst, supervisor, faculty member, and member of the president's council at the Center for Modern Psychoanalytic Studies. He is a member of the Society of Modern Psychoanalysts, the American Association of Marriage and Family Therapists, and the National Association for the Advancement of Psychoanalysis, where he has served as chairman of the accreditation committee and as administrative and research assistant to the president.

MOVAHEDI, SIAMAK, Ph.D., is a training and supervising analyst and director of the Institute for the Study of Psychoanalysis and Culture at the Boston Graduate School of Psychoanalysis. He is a professor of sociology at the University of Massachusetts, Boston.

PIEMONT, LISA, Ph.D., is a certified psychoanalyst in private practice in Summit, NJ. She is a member of the faculty at The Academy of Clinical and Applied Psychoanalysis (ACAP), and also serves as a fellow at the North Jersey Consultation Center, ACAP's clinical treatment service.

SHEPHERD, MARY, Psya.D., is a training and supervising analyst and a faculty member at the Boston Graduate School of Psychoanalysis. She has written on psychoanalytic research, the anaclitic countertransference, and the relationship between psychoanalysis and biology. Using biological and psychosocial data, Dr. Shepherd recently conducted empirical research that tested Hyman Spotnitz's hypothesis on the etiology of schizophrenia. She is in private practice in Cambridge and Brookline, MA.

YOUNG-BRUEHL, ELISABETH, Ph.D., is the author of the award-winning biographies *Hannah Arendt: For Love of the World* and *Anna Freud: A Biography*, and *Why Arendt Matters* in honor of Hannah Arendt's centenary in 2006. She has taught at Wesleyan University and at Haverford College and is currently living in Toronto, where she is a member of the Toronto Psychoanalytic Society. She is or has been on the editorial boards of numerous journals and continues to publish widely.